T0215904

Lecture Notes in Computer Science　　9591

Commenced Publication in 1973
Founding and Former Series Editors:
Gerhard Goos, Juris Hartmanis, and Jan van Leeuwen

More information about this series at http://www.springer.com/series/7410

Jan Camenisch · Doğan Kesdoğan (Eds.)

Open Problems in Network Security

IFIP WG 11.4 International Workshop, iNetSec 2015
Zurich, Switzerland, October 29, 2015
Revised Selected Papers

 Springer

Editors
Jan Camenisch
IBM Research Zurich
Rueschlikon
Switzerland

Doğan Kesdoğan
University of Regensburg
Regensburg
Germany

ISSN 0302-9743   ISSN 1611-3349 (electronic)
Lecture Notes in Computer Science
ISBN 978-3-319-39027-7 ISBN 978-3-319-39028-4 (eBook)
DOI 10.1007/978-3-319-39028-4

Library of Congress Control Number: 2016939100

LNCS Sublibrary: SL4 – Security and Cryptology

Preface

The international workshop iNetSec—Open Problems in Network Security—is the main workshop of the IFIP working group WG 11.4. Its objective is to present and discuss open problems and new research directions on all aspects related to network security.

Before 2009, iNetSec followed the traditional format where research papers were submitted, peer-reviewed, and then presented at the workshop. In 2009, this was changed into a format in which the discussion of open research problems and directions at the workshop becomes an integral part of the paper publication process. To enable this open workshop style yet remain focused on particular topics, we called for two-page abstracts in which the authors were asked to outline open research problems and new directions in network security. These abstracts were reviewed by the entire Program Committee, who ranked each of them according to whether the problem presented was relevant and suited for a discussion. At the workshop, we reserved almost as much time for each topic presentation as for its discussion, which was half an hour. After the workshop, the authors were asked to submit full papers based on their abstracts and the discussions at the workshop. These papers were reviewed and those with the highest ranks were selected for these proceedings. May they serve as a source of inspiration for new research!

We thank IBM Research – Zurich for hosting the workshop, the Program Committee for reviewing papers, as well as the authors of all submissions that enabled iNetSec 2015 to be take place. And last but not least, we are grateful to all participants for their contribution to the lively discussions.

April 2016

Jan Camenisch
Doğan Kesdoğan
Dang Vinh Pham

Organization

Executive Committee

Program Chairs

Jan Camenisch   IBM Research – Zurich, Switzerland
Doğan Kesdoğan   University of Regensburg, Germany

Organizing Chairs

Jan Camenisch   IBM Research – Zurich, Switzerland
Dang Vinh Pham   University of Regensburg, Germany

Program Committee

Jan Camenisch   IBM Research – Zurich, Switzerland
Hannes Federrath   University of Hamburg, Germany
Felix Freiling   Friedrich Alexander University FAU, Germany
Doğan Kesdoğan   University of Regensburg, Germany
Albert Levi   Sabanci University, Turkey
Javier Lopez   University of Malaga, Spain
Adrian Perrig   ETH Zurich, Switzerland
Dang Vinh Pham   University of Regensburg, Germany
Siraj A. Shaikh   Coventry University, UK

Contents

Network Security

Forwarding Accountability: A Challenging Necessity of the Future Data Plane

Christos Pappas[✉], Raphael M. Reischuk, and Adrian Perrig

ETH Zürich, Zurich, Switzerland
{pappasch,reischuk,adrian.perrig}@inf.ethz.ch

Abstract. Forwarding accountability mechanisms pinpoint the sending/forwarding properties of traffic to the entities that send and forward the traffic along a path. In this paper, we take flooding attacks as a use case and describe a proposal to hold senders accountable for the sending rates of their flows. Furthermore, we describe the corresponding challenges, potential solutions, and briefly present the literature in the area of forwarding accountability.

1 Introduction

The Internet started out as a small-scale network among scientists, and turned into a global-scale network for business and private communication alike. At the heart of this success story lies the best-effort delivery service of the network layer – a fundamental property of the Internet architecture. The network does neither provide guaranteed delivery of traffic, nor guaranteed quality of service. The simplicity of this design enabled multiple services and protocols to evolve on top of the minimalistic network layer.

Another property of the Internet architecture is the lack of feedback about the fate of packets. Functionality that detects whether and when packets were delivered is pushed to the end points without aid from the network. However, contrary to best-effort delivery, this design principle has raised trouble with respect to network security. To counter the problems of this design principle, we consider *forwarding accountability* a necessity for the future data plane.

In general, accountability mechanisms associate state and actions to entities, rendering misbehavior detectable, provable, and non-repudiable. Forwarding accountability in particular, associates the sending/forwarding properties of traffic (e.g., latency, bandwidth) to the entity that sends/forwards the traffic (e.g., a host, a router, a switch, or even an Autonomous System), constructing verifiable evidence about how traffic is sent/forwarded. This verifiable information can then be used by users or legal authorities to make informed decisions in cases of misbehavior or poorly performing networks entities.

In this paper, we highlight the importance of forwarding accountability by describing how it would aid in solving two burning issues for the networking community: network neutrality violations and flooding attacks.

© IFIP International Federation for Information Processing
Published by Springer International Publishing Switzerland 2016. All Rights Reserved
J. Camenisch and D. Kesdoğan (Eds.): iNetSec 2015, LNCS 9591, pp. 3–10, 2016.
DOI: 10.1007/978-3-319-39028-4_1

Network-Neutrality Violations. Network neutrality has become an increasingly hot subject in the networking community. Internet service providers (ISPs) have been accused of blocking [1,2] and slowing down traffic from specific content providers [4].

Consider the dispute between Netflix and Comcast [3]. Netflix – backed by the media and Internet activists – accused Comcast of deliberately slowing down its video traffic, causing an unacceptable quality of experience for the customers. Comcast denied the blame and attributed the problem to the inability of Netflix's direct ISPs to handle the amount of traffic.

An accountable data plane could alleviate many concerns raised by the neutrality debate [11]. As the exposed forwarding information would be trustworthy, the Internet community would obtain much richer feedback on how "neutral" an ISP really is. Verifiable information could be combined with other higher-level information (e.g., Service Level Agreements) to make an informed judgement about ISP's practices.

Flooding Attacks. In recent months, we have observed an increase in the frequency and intensity of flooding attacks rooted in misconfigured or vulnerable Internet services: in February 2014, attackers used misconfigured time synchronization servers to attack Cloudflare with a peak of 400 Gbps. For 2015, Akamai reports a 116.5 % increase in total DDoS attacks and a 42.8 % increase in the average attack duration compared to the previous year [5].

In an ideal Internet, users could enjoy the benefits of an accountable forwarding plane. Receivers could specify a traffic profile that sources need to adhere to, drawing a clear line for benign traffic and enabling misbehavior detection. In case of traffic profile violations, receivers could provide proofs of misbehavior to the origin and transit ISPs, and ISPs could ensure compliance for misbehaving hosts through traffic shaping.

We provide an example to demonstrate the virtues of forwarding accountability. Consider the topology depicted in Fig. 1 and assume that a web server is located in AS_n. We assume that an attacker launches a reflection attack against the server by exploiting the NTP protocol running on vulnerable servers in AS_0. Specifically, the attacker fakes the victim's source IP address and sends NTP commands to the servers within AS_0. Due to traffic amplification, the NTP servers generate traffic that overpowers the victim's resources.

With forwarding accountability in place, each packet is associated with a proof that can later remind every AS on the path that it forwarded the traffic. When the web server reports the attack to the ASes on the path by providing the per-packet proofs, the ASes can acknowledge or deny that they forwarded the malicious traffic. Based on the feedback from the ASes, it is possible to detect misbehavior and narrow down its location on the path. In our example, it becomes clear that the NTP servers in AS_0 sourced the malicious traffic. AS_0 can then drop or deprioritize AS_0's traffic and thus protect the victim web server and the other networks on the path.

Contributions. This paper's focus is on forwarding accountability with respect to flooding attacks. We extend our recent work, FAIR [12], by outlining an ACcountability-based Ddos Protection framework – ACDP – to hold the sending

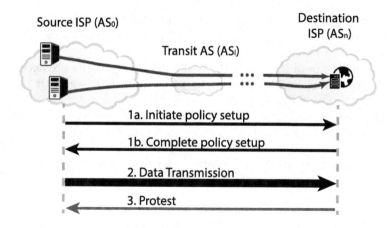

Fig. 1. ACDP operation.

hosts accountable for the sending rates of their originated flows. Furthermore, we describe the corresponding challenges and present the literature in the area of forwarding accountability.

2 Overview of ACDP

We provide a high-level overview of ACDP. In ACDP, communication proceeds in the following three stages (Fig. 1).

- **Stage 1 (Setup):** Source and destination hosts set up a sending policy that dictates the sending rate for a specific flow between them.
- **Stage 2 (Transmission):** The source sends its traffic to the destination. Each AS on the path (including the source's and destination's ISP) inscribes information in the packet headers, which serves as a reminder to itself that it has forwarded the packets.
- **Stage 3 (Protest):** If the destination host detects a sending-rate violation, it proceeds to the protest phase and hands the sending policy together with the packet headers to its own ISP. The ISP then contacts other ASes on the path by providing the aggregated proof; the proof eventually identifies the adversary.

2.1 Setup (Stage 1)

Before sending the actual data, communicating hosts set up a sending policy. The sending policy specifies the sending properties that a host should apply to its outgoing traffic towards the communicating peer. The sending properties can be formally expressed through the Token Bucket [8] parameters (the average sending rate, the maximum burst size, and the measurement interval). We consider bidirectional communication channels and thus, both communicating hosts indicate their preferred sending properties. Specifically, the sending policy is constructed as follows:

1. The source[1] initiates the policy setup and constructs a policy packet. It inscribes the sending properties that the destination should adhere to when sending traffic to the source.
2. Each AS on the path (including the host's ISP) indicates its presence on the path by inscribing its identifier in the policy packet. However, it does not interfere with the policy details.
3. The destination completes the policy by filling in its own desired sending properties that the source should adhere to. Then, it sends the policy packet back to the source.
4. Similar to step 2., each AS on the path back to the source – possibly different from the outbound path – indicates its presence.

We assume that communicating hosts sign their information with their private key, in order to make the policy non-repudiable. Furthermore, each AS uses a secret key to protect the integrity of its own information, so that it can later remind itself – without keeping state locally – that it witnessed the corresponding policy.

2.2   Transmission (Stage 2)

With the sending policy in place, hosts start exchanging traffic under the restrictions of the sending policy. We describe the data-plane operations performed by the source, transit, and destination ASes. These operations are applied to each packet.

Source AS. The border routers of the source AS inscribe the Autonomous System Number (ASN), a timestamp, and a sequence number. The timestamp is included to calculate the sending rate of the source in the next stage. Furthermore, in conjunction with the sequence number, it serves as a protection against packet replay from transit ASes. The ASN points to the AS that forwards a packet and constructs a trace of the AS path together with the ASNs of the next on-path ASes. Finally, the inscribed information is protected with a short MAC in the packet, computed with the secret key of the source AS.

Transit and Destination ASes. Each border router of the transit and destination ASes, performs the following operations:

1. The router verifies that the source's timestamp does not deviate from the local time. If the check fails, the packet gets dropped. This check ensures that the source AS does not collude with a customer host in order to conceal an attack by reporting false timestamps.
2. The router inscribes its own information in the packet: its ASN, a short nonce, and a MAC computed over the inscribed information. The nonce serves as protection against replaying the MAC of the AS.

---

[1] We refer to the host that initiates the connection as the source; and to its communicating peer as the destination.

The destination AS forwards the packet to the eventual recipient, who monitors each flow in order to detect policy violations. In case of a violation, the destination sends the received packets and the policy packet to its own ISP. The ISP proceeds to the protest phase, representing its customer.

2.3 Protest (Stage 3)

In the third stage, destination ASes provide proofs of misbehavior to the source AS and the other transit ASes. It is an offline procedure of at most two rounds.

In the first round, the destination AS sends the policy packet and the packet headers it received from its customer to the source AS. The policy packet contains the transmission properties, and the packet headers contain evidence about the actual transmission properties by the source. The source AS examines the evidence (i.e., verifies its own MAC inscribed in the packets) and approves or rejects the complaint. If the source AS approves the complaint, it can take measures against its misbehaving customer. However, a non-cooperating AS or a replay attack from a transit AS can lead to a rejected complaint in the first round.

A rejection in the first round leads to the second round. The destination AS sends the same information to all ASes on the path. They examine the evidence in the same way as the source AS and approve or reject the complaint. Based on the approvals and rejections, the ASes can determine the root of the problem, because each complaint is accepted at least by the benign cooperating ASes adjacent to the destination, as shown in FAIR [12].

3 Challenges

In this section, we discuss the major challenges related to our proposal. We sketch potential solutions and list the open problems to encourage future research with respect to deployment and performance.

3.1 Deployment Challenges

The first challenge is the required modification of hosts. With ACDP, end hosts have to perform additional functionality compared to the legacy communication paradigm (e.g., under TCP or UDP). Namely, end hosts have to perform a policy setup before a connection starts transmitting data. A change in the network stack of the host's operating system is an unrealistic requirement and we believe that this task can be delegated to a gateway between the host and its ISP. Typically, hosts connect to the Internet through their ISP-provided routers, which act as middleboxes and usually perform additional tasks (e.g., acting as a Network Address Translators or a firewall). Requiring middleboxes to interfere and perform the additional functionality keeps the hosts unmodified and provides a smoother deployment path.

A second challenge is the upgrade of the AS infrastructure required in order to inscribe the additional information in the packet headers; specifically, the MAC computation requires a hardware implementation of a cryptographic engine. Although it is impossible to circumvent this requirement, hardware crypto-graphic engines are readily available for commodity processors [10]. Since the required technology exists at a low price, the required upgrades would not incur a high procurement cost for ISPs.

The third challenge is a viable business model that provides incentives to ISPs to adopt such a mechanism. We anticipate that security-concerned cus-tomers (especially enterprise networks) will be interested in buying service from an ISP that handles and forwards its customers' complaints to the sources of misbehavior. Hence, competition would be the key to promote Accountability-as-a-Service [7]. However, a thorough economic analysis is required to explore the viability of such a security service.

3.2 Performance Challenges

The additional functionality required for ACDP introduces overhead with respect to processing, latency, and bandwidth.

A border router of an AS has to inscribe additional information, which includes the computation of a MAC. We conducted an experiment on one 10 GbE NIC port of a commodity server machine, simulating the required processing, and found that there was not a substantial drop in throughput. Specifically, for 64 byte packets (the minimum packet size, i.e., the maximum packet rate) the switch forwards at 95 % of the line-rate. For 128-byte packets and larger, the switch achieves line-rate performance. The initial results indicate that forward-ing performance would not suffer from such an accountability framework.

Another performance issue is the increase in latency for communicating hosts. Before the actual communication starts, end hosts must establish the sending policy, which translates to one Round-Trip-Time (RTT). This overhead can be significant for latency-sensitive applications (e.g., video streaming). More exten-sive research is required to optimize this aspect, but potential solutions include piggybacking the policy packet on the first data packets and embedding a default policy in the DNS records.

Our proposal comes with an increased packet size that leads to bandwidth overhead. The length increase is inevitable, but certain measures can limit the introduced overhead. For instance, a short MAC (4 bits) per ISP is enough to enable misbehavior detection in the context of flooding attacks [12].

4 Related Work

We present the main proposals in the area of forwarding accountability to date.

Goldberg et al. [9] propose end-to-end path quality monitoring in the pres-ence of adversaries. Specifically, an alarm is raised when packet loss and delay exceed a given threshold. The proposal leverages secure sampling, which allows end points to coordinate their measurements of loss and delay when an on-path adversary delays or drops packets. An alternative protocol uses a sketch to exchange loss measurements securely and efficiently in adversarial scenarios, accompanied by a theoretical analysis about their accuracy vs. overhead tradeoffs. In addition, these protocols make sensible assumptions for networking environments: no symmetric paths, no processing at forwarding devices, and configurable storage overhead based on accuracy target. However, these protocols do not provide granular performance reports for smaller path segments and do not localize misbehavior.

FAIR [12] is a forwarding accountability mechanism that pushes stricter security policies to ISPs. The source and destination ASes set up a communication channel with a corresponding sending policy, which can specify sending properties (e.g., average sending rate) or forbid abnormal packet headers used for malicious activity (e.g., Christmas tree packets). Transit ASes on the path mark packets and in case of policy violations, the packets are used as a proof of misbehavior. FAIR comes with an implementation that introduces low bandwidth overhead and can switch packets at a line-rate of 120 Gbps. However, the proposal does not allow proving misbehavior at the granularity of flows, and thus cannot be used to identify individual misbehaving flows or hosts.

AudIt [6] proposes an accountability interface, provided by ISPs, that gives loss and delay feedback to the traffic sources. The framework relies on statistics reports from ISPs, without requiring complicated key establishment. However, the proposal is based on aggregation of flow information, and thus ISPs can hide their lies since they report mean values.

References

1. FCC Fines Telecom that Blocked Vonage VoIP Calls, March 2005. http://bit.ly/1MokIA4
2. AT&T Faces Formal FCC Complaint for Blocking Cellular FaceTime Use, September 2012. http://bit.ly/1JYNxpt
3. Comcast vs. Netflix: Is This Really About Net Neutrality? May 2014. http://cnet.co/T6JuPP
4. Netflix Performance on Verizon and Comcast Has Been Dropping for Months, February 2014. http://bit.ly/1URc8zR
5. Akamai: Q1 State of the Internet - Security Report (2015). http://bit.ly/1RhrFWs
6. Argyraki, K., Maniatis, P., Irzak, O., Ashish, S., Shenker, S.: Loss and delay accountability for the internet. In: Proceedings of ICNP, October 2007
7. Bender, A., Spring, N., Levin, D., Bhattacharjee, B.: Accountability as a service. In: Proceedings of the 3rd USENIX Workshop on Steps to Reducing Unwanted Traffic on the Internet, pp. 5: 1–5: 6. SRUTI 2007. USENIX Association, Berkeley, CA, USA (2007). http://dl.acm.org/citation.cfm?id=1361436.1361441
8. Cisco: Cisco Policing and Shaping Overview, May 2015. http://bit.ly/1HOHr9V
9. Goldberg, S., Xiao, D., Tromer, E., Barak, B., Rexford, J.: Path-quality Monitoring in the Presence of Adversaries. In: Proceedings of ACM SIGMETRICS (2008)

10. Gueron, S.: Intel Advanced Encryption Standard (AES) New Instruction Set, March 2010. https://software.intel.com/sites/default/files/article/165683/aes-wp-2012-09-22-v01.pdf
11. Pappas, C., Argyraki, K., Bechtold, S., Adrian, P.: Transparency instead of neutrality. In: Proceedings of ACM HotNets, November 2015
12. Pappas, C., Reischuk, R.M., Perrig, A.: FAIR: forwarding accountability for internet reputability. In: Proceedings of IEEE ICNP, November 2015

A Metric for Adaptive Routing
on Trustworthy Paths

Christoph Hofmann[1](✉), Elke Franz[1], and Silvia Santini[2]

[1] Chair of Privacy and Data Security,
Technische Universität Dresden, 01062 Dresden, Germany
{christoph.hofmann,elke.franz}@tu-dresden.de
[2] Chair of Embedded Systems,
Technische Universität Dresden, 01062 Dresden, Germany
silvia.santini@tu-dresden.de

Abstract. Any data transmission over multiple hops requires the use of routing algorithms to find a path from the sender to the receiver(s). Supporting secure data transmissions further requires the selected path to be trustworthy, i.e., not under the control of an attacker. Since attacks can occur at any time during data transmission, the current state of the network must be considered when selecting trustworthy paths. In this paper, we introduce a novel metric – called *Locally Evaluated Trust* (LET) – for local trust evaluation. The LET metric can be used by adaptive routing algorithms to select a trustworthy path. To evaluate our approach, we simulate different routing algorithms and compare their performance in the presence of one or more malicious nodes in a two-dimensional torus mesh. Our results show that the LET metric allows adaptive routing algorithms to effectively identify and circumvent malicious nodes.

Keywords: Adaptive routing · Attacker model · Trustworthiness · Local trust rating

1 Introduction

Data transmission in a communication network requires the use of routing algorithms to find a path from the sender to the receiver(s). Common requirements on routing algorithms are a minimal path length, high throughput, and low latency. Adaptive routing algorithms allow to consider the current state of the network in order to achieve these goals.

To select a path, existing algorithms often evaluate efficiency metrics such as the current load of neighboring nodes or the quality of links. But besides efficiency, the security of data transmission is also essential. A routing algorithm should thus be able to efficiently deliver packets to the intended recipients even in the presence of attackers.

An attacker may disturb the transmission in several ways, for instance by dropping or delaying packets. The sender can however typically detect whether

J. Camenisch and D. Kesdoğan (Eds.): iNetSec 2015, LNCS 9591, pp. 11–25, 2016.
DOI: 10.1007/978-3-319-39028-4_2

a data transmission has been successful or not by using acknowledgments – short messages sent by the recipient to the sender upon the reception of a data transmission. If an acknowledgment is not received within a pre-specified time interval, the routing algorithm assumes the message (or the acknowledgment) was lost. Lost messages are then often retransmitted but retransmissions increase network load, power consumption, and communication latency. To prevent attackers from causing this overhead, routing algorithms should thus select trustworthy paths. To prevent new attack possibilities and to limit the communication overhead, the selection of trustworthy paths should neither require the participation of a central entity in the network nor the exchange of information about possible attacks or attackers.

In this paper, we propose a novel metric to evaluate the trustworthiness of network nodes in a decentralized fashion. Our metric, called LET (Locally Evaluated Trust), is designed to guide the choice of trustworthy paths in adaptive routing algorithms. Every node in the network evaluates the trustworthiness of its one-hop neighbors using information about received (or missed) acknowledgments. Thereby, a missing acknowledgment lowers the trustworthiness of a neighbor and of every path passing through it. The lower the trustworthiness of a neighbor, the lower is the probability for this neighbor to be included in a routing path (and vice versa).

To evaluate the effectiveness of our metric, we implement four routing algorithms and simulate their behavior under the presence of one or more malicious nodes. Our results show that LET can describe the trustworthiness of paths even if it is based solely on local information about adjacent nodes. Algorithms that leverage our metric achieve a significant higher rate of successfully delivered packets in comparison to other algorithms.

The remainder of the paper is organized as follows. We review related work in Sect. 2. In Sect. 3, we describe our system model as well as the attacker model and introduce the LET metric. Section 4 describes our evaluation setup and the results of our simulations. Finally, Sect. 5 concludes the paper and provides an outlook on future work.

2   Related Work

The selection of a suitable path from a given source to a destination is the essential task of every routing algorithm. Based on the way algorithms select a routing path, they can be classified as deterministic, oblivious, or adaptive algorithms [4]. XY routing and Valliant's routing algorithm are examples for deterministic or oblivious routing algorithms. Both are based on the model of Dimension Order Routing (DOR) where packets are routed ordered by direction until they reach the closest point to the destination or the destination itself [4].

Deterministic and oblivious algorithms select a path only based on predefined rules. In contrast, adaptive algorithms are able to consider information about the current state of the network. This characteristic of routing algorithms is of course also necessary to select a trustworthy path.

Information about the current state of the network are described by means of metrics. Baumann et al. [1] give an overview about metrics for different purposes.

Several metrics evaluate the efficiency of a path using various methods. A well known and often used metric is the minimum hop count which always selects a shortest path from source to destination. But selecting a minimal path is not reasonable all the time, especially if packet loss can occur during the transmission. In wired networks, packet loss is usually caused by congestion. The Transmission Control Protocol (TCP) was designed to cope with these problems in wired networks. Since packet losses indicate congestion, fewer packets are sent until the problems diminish.

In wireless networks, however, packet loss is usually caused by a bad quality of the links. Retransmissions are then used to recover from packet losses. Several metrics for the description of the quality of links have been proposed for Wireless Sensor Networks (WSN) and Mobile Ad-hoc Networks (MANETs).

A well known example is the Expected Transmission Count (ETX) [5]. The ETX of a link is an estimate of the number of packet transmissions that are necessary to deliver a packet from one node to the next. ETX is computed by considering information about the delivery ratio of previously sent data and control packets. The ETX of a path from a sender to a destination can then be computed as the sum of the ETX values for each link on the path.

ETX has been used also in the context of wireless sensor networks. For instance, Gnawali et al. [10] use the ETX to guide the construction of a collection tree along which packets are routed towards one or more sinks. Thereby, the next forwarder for a given packet is determined in a hop-by-hop fashion, i.e., the neighbor with the smallest ETX is chosen as the next hop. Generic routing algorithms for wireless sensor networks also use other metrics, like the EDC (Expected Duty Cycle) proposed in [12]. This metric enables the ORW (Opportunistic Routing in Wireless sensor network) protocol to select routes in the network in an opportunistic way, thereby minimizing the overall time during which nodes have their radios switched on. A number of other approaches and metrics have been presented in the wireless sensor networks literature, e.g. [7]. They however mainly focus on improving reliability and latency while minimizing energy consumption. Security issues are instead often neglected.

However, security of transmission is also essential. A maliciously acting node may launch several kinds of attacks, either alone or in cooperation with other malicious nodes. Such attacks like modifying packets, selective forwarding of packets, or sinkhole and blackhole attacks where packets are dropped can harm the network massively and have a severe influence on routing performance [6,11]. Therefore, it should be possible to determine, identify, and circumvent these maliciously acting nodes. The routing algorithm should be able to select a trustworthy path that is not under the control of an attacker.

At first sight, it should be possible to use a metric that describes the quality of links also for the description of the trustworthiness, since both a bad link quality and active attacks may cause packet loss and require retransmission of packets. However, as Dong et al. discussed in [6], a metric that only focuses on maximizing the throughput can also introduce new attack possibilities. For example, nodes can try to manipulate local metrics as well as global metrics in order to manipulate and control traffic. Another difference between routing in the presence of faults and in the presence of attackers is the question what is an adequate strategy to react on problems. In case of faults, the routing algorithm can still try to send packets over the path, maybe sending additional redundant packets, before an alternative path is selected. In case of malicious nodes, the routing algorithm should try to select a trustworthy path as soon as possible.

Another direction of research that directly considers malicious nodes is to apply reputation as basis for a metric. One example is a metric called CORE [14] that proposes a mechanism to rate the willingness of a node to cooperate in the network. Each node keeps a list containing the reputation of his adjacent neighbors. The overall reputation is calculated by subjective and indirect reputation and ranges from −1 (bad) to +1 (good). Subjective reputation is based on the nodes' own observations whereas indirect reputation is based on observations made by other nodes. Nodes that are not cooperating are penalized by bad reputation. Other examples for reputation based metrics are described in [2] and [16]. They also propose trust evaluation based on direct observations and information which is propagated by other nodes in the network.

A further approach for rating the trustworthiness is described in [13] for MANETs. A watchdog mechanism and a pathrater are defined to describe the reliability of a neighbor node. Nodes store information about recently sent packets in a buffer and use the watchdog mechanism to overhear the communication of their neighboring nodes by using the promiscuous mode. If a node notices that a formerly sent packet was forwarded by its neighbor correctly, the packet is removed from the buffer. Otherwise, if a packet remains in the buffer longer than a certain period, the responsible neighbor node gets a bad reputation. This mechanism is performed by every node on the path. If a node observes bad behavior of its neighboring node, it accuses this node to the source of the packet.

However, similar problems are relevant for metrics based on reputation as discussed in [6] for high-throughput metrics. If notifications about the misbehavior of nodes or accusations are used for the computation of the metric, an attacker can try to manipulate the metric. To cope with these problems, Dong et al. suggested a measurement-based detection of attacks combined with a temporary accusation-based reaction [6]. To limit the abuse of the accusation, nodes can only issue a new accusation after the previously issued one expired.

In the approach we introduce in this paper, we aim at excluding attacks that utilize indirect information delivered by other nodes such as probe packets, notifications, or accusations. Therefore, the proposed metric is solely based on local observations what additionally minimizes the overall communication overhead. The metric can be used by an adaptive routing algorithm that aims at selecting trustworthy paths.

A similar approach was introduced in [9,15]. The authors also discuss ratings based on local observations by means on end-to-end acknowledgments. The main difference to our approach is the fact that senders and forwarders rate their neighbors what requires that the acknowledgments are sent back using the reverse path. In contrast, we aim at a solution that does not impose overhead to the forwarders. Hence, rating is only done by the senders. Forwarders do not have to keep track of the success of forwarding data packets. Further, this also means that we do not need a special treatment of acknowledgments, they can be routed like data packets. Since we assume a system with a high volume of data traffic, all nodes will act as sender and rate their neighbors after a short time. A further difference is the system topology. While the authors of [9,15] discuss ad hoc networks, we assume a fixed topology where the possible paths to the recipient are known from the beginning. This fixed topology allows to study different constellations of malicious nodes.

3   Our Approach

3.1   System Model

In this work we focus on a two-dimensional torus topology. This topology is found in several systems like for instance the HAEC Box (Highly Adaptive Energy-Efficient Computing), a novel high performance computing platform that is currently under development at TU Dresden [8].

The HAEC Box consists of several stacked boards each endowed with powerful compute nodes that cooperate to execute parallel applications. Nodes on each board are connected through optical waveguides in a two-dimensional torus. Each node can directly communicate with the compute nodes of adjacent boards by means of wireless links. During the execution of an application on the HAEC Box, compute nodes are expected to communicate intensively with each other. Hence, the efficiency of routing has a significant influence on the overall performance of the HAEC Box. In

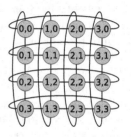

Fig. 1. 4×4 torus mesh

this paper, we focus on the topology of a single board, i.e., on a regular torus mesh network with m rows and n columns as illustrated in Fig. 1.

Further, we focus on unicast communication where one sender communicates with one receiver over one or more intermediate nodes (forwarders). Each node can be a sender, forwarder, or receiver. Receivers issue acknowledgments to inform the sender about the successful delivery of data packets. These end-to-end acknowledgments are routed through the network as data packets.

3.2   Attacker Model

In this work, we consider only active attackers. Active attackers can, e.g., modify or drop packets (data packets as well as acknowledgments), delay their transmission or replay formerly sent packets. The presence of these attackers can thus be detected using quantitative metrics. For instance, an increase in the average data delivery latency might hint at the presence of an attacker who delays packets.

Passive attackers only observe the data transmitted. However, as long as an attacker only observes, it is not possible to recognize the attack and, hence, not possible to describe it in a metric. The confidentiality of the data can, however, be enforced through end-to-end encryption. We therefore assume the use of end-to-end encryption and do not further discuss passive attacks.

We further assume that appropriate security measures like digital signatures are in place that enable nodes to verify the origin and validity of received packets. Hence, modified packets can be recognized and will be discarded so that a modification implies a packet loss as well. Therefore, we do not explicitly distinguish between modification and dropping of packets in the following.

The sender recognizes the loss of a packet if a data transmission is not acknowledged within a pre-defined time interval (timeout). Since it is not possible to distinguish whether the data packet or the acknowledgment was lost, both cases are treated as the same. The delay of a transmission can also cause the detection of a packet loss, but when the acknowledgment eventually reaches the sender, this false detection can be corrected. The replay of acknowledgments to conceal an attack is not possible since we assume that the acknowledgment is digitally signed by the receiver and contains a unique reference to the acknowledged data packet.

An active attacker can also affect network availability by flooding the network with useless traffic (denial of service). The LET metric considers the trustworthiness of nodes and is not designed for this type of attacks. Thus, it is not helpful to prevent or detect them. We leave the consideration of denial of service attacks to future work.

We assume that both links or nodes may be attacked. Since the implications are the same, we model the active attacker by one or more malicious nodes. Malicious nodes drop packets with a certain probability (selective forwarding) or drop all packets in total (sinkhole attack). As we mentioned before, this packet dropping also covers the modification of packets.

Participants of a communication are the sender, the forwarder(s) and the receiver. Regarding the role of the attacker, we can distinguish different cases.

- *Only forwarders can be malicious:* Senders and receivers are trustworthy, they want to protect their communication. We assume that malicious nodes only want to disturb the traffic, they do not act as sender or receiver.
- *Forwarders and receivers can be malicious:* The receiving node may be controlled by an attacker and, therefore, malicious. In this case, the receiver does not send back an acknowledgment. Again, malicious nodes are only interested in disturbing the communication between other nodes and do not act as sender.
- *Senders, forwarders, and receivers can be malicious:* Malicious nodes are interested in disturbing the communication between other nodes, but they also want to communicate themselves.

For our first evaluations, we consider the first case. We mainly focus on malicious nodes that drop all packets but also consider malicious nodes that perform selective forwarding.

3.3   Locally Evaluated Trust (LET) Metric

In our approach, each node locally rates the trustworthiness of its four neighboring nodes (north, east, south, and west) by evaluating the delivery of previously sent packets. This implies that LET does not apply to a whole path but only to adjacent nodes. Before transmitting a packet, the sender and each forwarder consider their locally computed trust values to select the next node on the path.

The range for the trust value can be arbitrary. For the sake of simplicity, we let the LET range between 0 (untrusted) and 1 (trusted). A trust value of 0.5 indicates a neutral rating that is also used as the initial value of the metric.

Updates of the LET are triggered by local observations of the nodes. For each sent packet, the sender logs the identifier of the packet, the time of transmission, and the identifier of the neighbor that was selected as successor. The reception of an acknowledgment confirms the successful delivery of that packet. The sender does not know the path that was used, but knows that the node it selected as first forwarder processed the packet correctly. Hence, the acknowledgment triggers a positive rating of that neighbor.

On the other side, a missing acknowledgment indicates a problem, although the sender cannot identify the reason. The loss of a data packet or of the corresponding acknowledgment could have been caused by an attacker or by a fault in the network. The sender only knows to which of its neighbors it has sent the packet and, therefore, decreases the rating of that neighbor. This might be "unfair" since the neighbor may not be the cause of the problem. In this case, further successful routing over this node will improve its rating again.

LET values are updated as follows:

$$up\,(trust) = \begin{cases} trust + trust & \text{for } trust < 0.5 \\[2mm] trust + \dfrac{1 - trust}{2} & \text{for } trust \geq 0.5 \end{cases}$$

$$down\,(trust) = \begin{cases} trust - \dfrac{trust}{2} & \text{for } trust \leq 0.5 \\[2mm] trust - (1 - trust) & \text{for } trust > 0.5 \end{cases}$$

If a node changes its behavior, the metric should reflect this change as soon as possible. For our evaluation, we use static intervals and restricted the number of possible trust values to five positive and five negative ratings (Fig. 2).

3.4   Path Selection

To prevent problems of adaptive routing algorithms like deadlocks or livelocks, we use the Odd-Even-Turn-Model [3] as a basic path selection method. This model restricts the movements of a packet to certain allowed turns depending on the x coordinate of the node that takes the routing decision. These restrictions prevent cycles in the routing path and thus livelocks to occur.

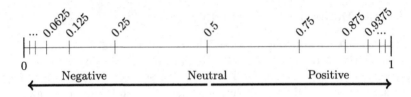

Fig. 2. Range of the trust value

In our decentralized adaptive approach, each forwarder selects the next node on the path to the receiver. To guide this selection, we first follow the rules of the Odd-Even-Turn-Model. The set of nodes that are not excluded by this model establish the set of *available nodes* (Av). Since we are also interested in selecting a short path, the neighbors that are on a minimal path to the receiver are selected from the available nodes ($Av_{min} \subseteq Av$).

We then consider the LET value computed by each node to further refine the choice of the next node. Simply selecting the node with the highest LET is however not beneficial. First, this node might become overloaded and thus cause latency to increase. Second, choosing always the node with the highest LET as the next successor prevents other nodes from getting the chance to improve their reputation by participating in a data transmission. Third, if the LET of available nodes that allow the selection of a minimal path are equal, we select one of these nodes at random irrespectively of the actual LET value.

We accordingly define two thresholds to classify the trustworthiness of the available nodes providing minimal paths. We refer to nodes with $trust \geq 0.5$ as *high trust nodes* ($Av_{min,h} \subseteq Av_{min}$) and to nodes with $0.06 \leq trust < 0.5$ as *low trust nodes* ($Av_{min,l} \subseteq Av_{min}$). The definition of these sets increases the chance for a node to be selected as successor and, thus, to get the opportunity to improve its rating. The node that makes the routing decision selects a high trust neighbor from the set $Av_{min,h}$. If there is no high trust neighbor ($Av_{min,h} = \emptyset$), the node selects a low trust neighbor from $Av_{min,l}$. If there is also no low trust neighbor ($Av_{min,l} = \emptyset$), the node selects the neighbor with the highest trust value from the set of available nodes (Av). In this latter case, the chosen neighbor does not lie on a minimal path.

4   Evaluation

4.1   Simulation

We simulated four routing algorithms in a 4×4 torus mesh network:

XY: Static XY routing,
OE$_l$: Odd-Even-Routing [3] with the current load as a metric,
OE$_t$: Odd-Even-Routing [3] with the proposed LET metric,
OE$_o$: Own implementation of the Odd-Even-Turn-Model with the proposed LET metric.

Two of these algorithms (OE_t, OE_o) apply the suggested LET metric, the other ones (XY, OE_l) serve as a reference. OE_o is an own implementation of the Odd-Even-Turn-Model since the implementation of this model given in [3] excludes some turns that are not forbidden by the Odd-Even-Turn-Model itself.

The simulation was done with Python using the discrete-event simulation framework SimPy [17], which allows a discrete time basis for the simulation. In our simulation, a node is able to process one packet per discrete time step (called tick in the following). At each node, incoming packets are stored in a queue and processed in a FIFO order.

The aim of our simulation was to observe the behavior of the four routing algorithms under the presence of one or more malicious nodes. A maliciously acting node either drops all packets given to it or selectively forwards them with a certain probability. To enable a fair comparison, each of the four routing algorithms is simulated in a separate mesh with identical settings for the selection of the malicious nodes and probabilities in case of selective forwarding. In every tick, a packet with random sender and receiver is created and given to each mesh.

We simulated different scenarios regarding number and constellation of malicious nodes. For each scenario, we performed 10 simulation runs with 10000 packets each. Preliminary tests have confirmed that this number of packets is sufficient to achieve a sufficiently small standard deviation of the results. During the simulation, the efficiency parameters described in the next section are determined and averaged over all runs.

4.2 Evaluation Parameters

The performance of the simulated routing algorithms was evaluated by a comparison of different evaluation parameters. One of these parameters is the *Delivery Ratio* that reflects the ability of the routing algorithm to deliver packets even in the presence of malicious nodes.

Another interesting parameter is the average total load (*AvrLoad*), which reflects the overall load of the network. We compute the load of a single node by the length of its queue and the total load of a path as sum of the loads of all nodes on that path. The load has a significant influence on the average time (*AvrTime*) needed to route a packet. Both *AvrLoad* and *AvrTime* can only be computed in relation to the delivered packets.

4.3 Results and Discussion

In first experiments, we assumed that malicious nodes drop all packets (sinkhole attacks). Figure 3 compares the delivery ratios of the routing algorithms for different numbers and constellations of malicious nodes.

In case the network contains only one misbehaving malicious node, all algorithms can deliver more than 90 % of the packets. Adding more malicious nodes to the network decreases the delivery ratio of algorithms not using our proposed

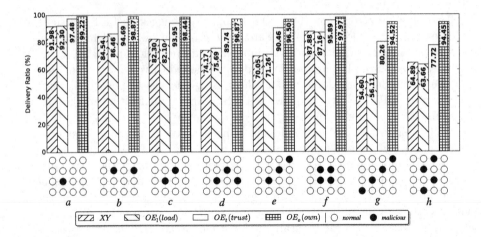

Fig. 3. Delivery ratios for different constellations of malicious nodes

trust metric massively. In the case of three malicious nodes arranged diagonally in the network (e), the delivery ratios of XY and OE_l only reach around 70 %, whereas the algorithms using the LET metric still perform good reaching 90 % (OE_t) and 96 % (OE_o). Adding one more malicious node to the diagonal arrangement (g) causes the delivery ratio of XY and OE_l get even worse. Almost the half of all sent packets cannot reach their designated destinations in this scenario. While the delivery ratio of OE_t also drops by around 10 %, the delivery ratio of our own implemented version of the Odd-Even-Turn-Model still reaches a good performance of 94 %. This can be explained by the greater number of routing options offered by the own implementation.

Furthermore, we found out that the performance does not depend on the number of malicious nodes only. The arrangement of malicious nodes also has a significant influence on the results. While the algorithms reach relatively high delivery ratios in a network with four malicious nodes arranged in the middle of the mesh (f), the algorithms may already behave worse in a network with only two malicious nodes (e.g., c). This is mainly due to the fact that in the case of arrangement f, where malicious nodes are located in the center of the network, all honest nodes have only one misbehaving neighbor, whereas in case of arrangement c four nodes have one malicious neighbor and two nodes even have to deal with two malicious neighbors.

That also explains the low delivery ratios in constellations g and h. In arrangement g, eight honest nodes have to deal with two malicious neighbors. In case of arrangement h, four nodes have one malicious neighbor and four other nodes even have to deal with three malicious neighbors. If a node has three malicious neighbors, there is only one trustworthy link. In case of attackers that drop all packets, such a node can only send or receive packets. If the node has to forward a packet, it will always be dropped by one of its malicious neighbors.

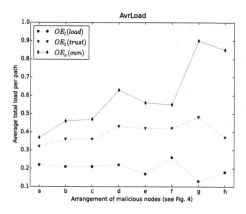

Fig. 4. Average total load per path for each arrangement

Another interesting parameter for evaluating the different approaches is the average load (**AvrLoad**). Figure 4 shows the average load on a path for each of the malicious node constellations presented in Fig. 3.

As the average load can only be calculated for successfully delivered packets, the values to some extend depend on the delivery ratios. This means that in the case of a lower delivery ratio the values base on fewer measurements and therefore are less meaningful. Nevertheless, it appears that the average load is constantly low for the Odd-Even algorithm using the load as a metric (OE_l).

Regarding the algorithms that use the trustworthiness as a metric (OE_t and OE_o), the average load is increasing according to the number of malicious nodes in the network. While the delivery ratio of OE_o is more or less constantly high, the average load increases rapidly from about 0.4 (one malicious node) to about 0.9 (four malicious nodes). This can be explained through the limitations imposed by the malicious nodes in the network. They force the nodes to use one of the few remaining trustworthy paths in the network for routing a packet. This causes higher load on these paths.

The average time needed to transmit a packet (**AvrTime**) is closely related to the average load on a path. Figure 5 shows that the average time for routing a packet using OE_o increases with the number of malicious nodes. This is mainly due to the fact that the load and therefore the time a packet has to wait to get routed also increases. In addition, OE_o allows non-minimal routing paths in the absence of a minimal path with a certain trustworthiness. A non-minimal path also increases the time needed for routing. For OE_t, the average time remains mainly constant whereas the average time for OE_l decreases. Again, these values also depend on the delivery ratio since the average time can only be calculated for successfully delivered packets. The number of malicious nodes significantly influences the delivery ratio of OE_l. In case of many attackers, only packets with a receiver close to the sender are routed successfully. Therefore, the path length is short and the average time decreases.

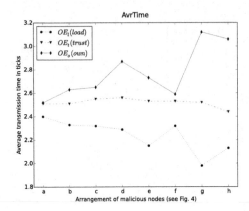

Fig. 5. Average time in ticks for the transmission of a packet

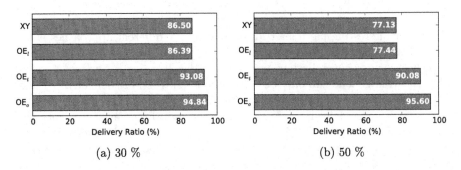

Fig. 6. Delivery ratio for selective forwarding malicious nodes

As described in our attacker model, a maliciously acting node may only forward some of the packets it receives. The rest is dropped. This malicious behavior is also known as selective forwarding. We also tested the LET metric under the presence of nodes that drop packets with a certain probability. Figure 6 shows the delivery ratios for a network with four malicious nodes dropping packets with a probability of 30 % (a) or 50 % (b). The malicious nodes were arranged as shown in constellation g (see Fig. 3).

Also in case of selective forwarding nodes, the two algorithms using our proposed metric (OE_t and OE_o) outperform the other tested algorithms. These results confirm that the metric is able to identify and circumvent the misbehaving nodes even if they only drop parts of the traffic. Of course, the detection of malicious nodes is more complicated in comparison to sinkhole attacks and, therefore, takes more time.

Figure 7 shows the ratings performed by each node for a simulation with one malicious node. A gray box represents a positive rating while a black box indicates a negative rating. Ratings are ordered chronologically in the direction of the arrow. Thus, boxes closer to the rating node imply an earlier rating.

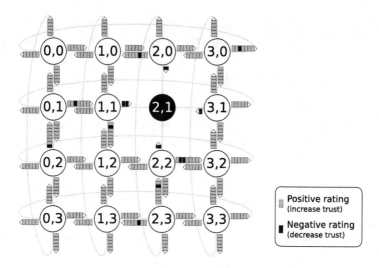

Fig. 7. Trust ratings performed in a network with one malicious node

This presentation of the ratings shows that all neighbors of the malicious node (2,1) were able to determine its malicious behavior. Because of alternative paths with good reputation, the decreased connections are not used anymore. An exception is the second negative rating of node (1,1): node (2,1) was selected as first forwarder by node (1,1) again before the time out for the first lost packet was reached.

As discussed earlier, a timeout can also falsely cause a negative rating since the sender cannot localize the reason of a packet loss. However, if a falsely decreased but honest node is used again, it will improve it's trust value.

4.4 Limitations

One limitation of our approach is that a rating is only issued by senders. As long as a node only acts as forwarder or receiver, it does not have the possibility to rate its neighbors. However, under the assumption of a high traffic volume, this issue is not crucial.

Another point to be considered is that we assume honest senders and receivers in our simulations. While a malicious sender that behaves selfishly and does not forward packets but sends own packets is not a problem, a malicious receiver that constantly refuses to send acknowledgments affects a proper establishment of trust on sender side.

Since it is not possible to identify the reason of a timeout of an acknowledgment, the sender decreases the trust value of the selected successor. However, if that node processed the packet correctly, this downgrade is not justified.

Due to the high connectivity of the torus mesh, it may take some time before a wrongly degraded node will be selected as forwarder again. Either other available nodes are downgraded to the same trust level (low trust nodes), or the sender improves the trust value of the falsely accused node. The latter is only possible if the sender has to send a packet directly to this neighbor.

5   Summary and Outlook

Within this paper, we presented a novel metric (LET) for trust evaluation. Our proposed metric only utilizes local observations for the establishment of trust values. Simulations confirmed that adaptive algorithms using our proposed metric can successfully identify and circumvent misbehaving nodes. As a consequence, these algorithms are able to achieve higher delivery ratios in comparison to other routing algorithms. Furthermore, the simulations showed that the arrangement of malicious nodes in the network has a significant impact on the performance of the algorithms.

Besides cryptographic mechanisms like encryption, consideration of the trustworthiness provides a proactive method to protect packets in a communication network.

Until now, we only utilized end-to-end acknowledgments for trust evaluation. A topic of future work is to investigate the use of link-to-link acknowledgments. Even if link-to-link acknowledgments will increase the overall communication overhead, they may enhance the accuracy of the metric. Further, they allow to overcome the limitation that only senders can issue ratings. Of course, potential new attacks have to be carefully investigated as well. For future work, we will consider the usage of dynamic rating intervals to further improve the rating process and to ensure that LET reflects a changed node behavior as soon as possible. Another topic of future work is to study the influence of more dynamic attackers that change their behavior over time and to improve the rating accordingly. Future simulations will also consider other possible roles of the attacker (malicious sender or receiver) as mentioned in Sect. 3.2. Finally, we will investigate the performance of our metric in other topologies. First experiments for a slightly bigger 8×8 torus mesh network delivered promising results.

Acknowledgments. This work is partly supported by the German Research Foundation (DFG) in the CRC 912 "Highly Adapted Energy-Efficient Computing". Further, the authors wish to thank the anonymous reviewers for their helpful comments.

References

1. Baumann, R., Heimlicher, S., Strasser, M., Weibel, A.: A Survey on Routing Metrics. TIK report 262 (2007)
2. Buchegger, S., Le Boudec, J.-Y.: Performance analysis of the CONFIDANT protocol. In: Proceedings of the 3rd ACM International Symposium on Mobile A Hoc Networking & Computing, pp. 226–236. ACM (2002)
3. Chiu, G.-M.: The odd-even turn model for adaptive routing. IEEE Trans. Parallel Distrib. Syst. **11**(7), 729–738 (2000)
4. Dally, W.J., Towles, B.P.: Principles and Practices of Interconnection Networks. Elsevier, San Mateo (2004)

5. De Couto, D.S., Aguayo, D., Bicket, J., Morris, R.: A high-throughput path metric for multi-hop wireless routing. Wireless Netw. **11**(4), 419–434 (2005)
6. Dong, J., Curtmola, R., Nita-Rotaru, C.: On the pitfalls of high-throughput multicast metrics in adversarial wireless mesh networks. In: Proceedings of the IEEE SECON, pp. 224–232 (2008)
7. Duquennoy, S., Landsiedel, O., Voigt, T.: Let the tree bloom: scalable opportunistic routing with ORPL. In: Proceedings of the 11th ACM Conference on Embedded Networked Sensor Systems (SenSys) (2013)
8. Fettweis, G., Nagel, W.E., Lehner, W.: Pathways to servers of the future. In: Proceedings of the DATE (2012)
9. Galuba, W., Papadimitratos, P., Poturalski, M., Aberer, K., Despotovic, Z., Kellerer, W.: Castor: scalable secure routing for ad hoc networks. In: Proceedings of the IEEE INFOCOMM 2010 (2010)
10. Gnawali, O., Fonseca, R., Jamieson, K., Moss, D., Levis, P.: Collection tree protocol. In: Proceedings of the 7th ACM Conference on Embedded Networked Sensor Systems (SenSys) (2009)
11. Karlof, C., Wagner, D.: Secure routing in wireless sensor networks: attacks and countermeasures. Ad hoc Netw. **1**(2), 293–315 (2003)
12. Landsiedel, O., Ghadimi, E., Duquennoy, S., Johansson, M., Power, L., Delay, L.: Opportunistic routing meets duty cycling. In: Proceedings of the Conference on Information Processing in Sensor Networks (ACM/IEEE IPSN) (2012)
13. Marti, S., Giuli, T.J., Lai, K., Baker, M.: Mitigating routing misbehavior in mobile ad hoc networks. In: Proceedings of the 6th Annual International Conference on Mobile Computing and Networking, pp. 255–265. ACM (2000)
14. Michiardi, P., Molva, R.: CORE: a collaborative reputation mechanism to enforce node cooperation in mobile ad hoc networks. In: Jerman-Blažič, B., Klobučar, T. (eds.) Advanced Communications and Multimedia Security. IFIP, vol. 100, pp. 107–121. Springer, Heidelberg (2002)
15. Papadimitratos, P., Haas, Z.J.: Secure data communication in mobile ad hoc networks. IEEE JSAG **24**(2), 343–356 (2006)
16. Rezgui, A., Eltoweissy, M.: TARP: a trust-aware routing protocol for sensor-actuator networks. In: Proceedings of the IEEE International Conference on Mobile Adhoc and Sensor Systems, pp. 1–9. IEEE (2007)
17. SimPy. simpy.readthedocs.org

Intrusion Detection

Early Warning Systems for Cyber Defence

Harsha Kalutarage[1]([⊠]), Siraj Shaikh[2], Bu-Sung Lee[3], Chonho Lee[3],
and Yeo Chai Kiat[3]

[1] The Centre for Secure Information Technologies,
Queen's University of Belfast, Belfast, UK
h.kalutarage@qub.ac.uk
[2] The Centre for Mobility and Transport, Coventry University, Coventry, UK
s.shaikh@coventry.ac.uk
[3] Nanyang Technological University, Singapore, Singapore
{ebslee,leechonho,asckyeo}@ntu.edu.sg

Abstract. Cybercriminals ramp up their efforts with sophisticated techniques while defenders gradually update their typical security measures. Attackers often have a long-term interest in their targets. Due to a number of factors such as scale, architecture and nonproductive traffic however it makes difficult to detect them using typical intrusion detection techniques. Cyber early warning systems (CEWS) aim at alerting such attempts in their nascent stages using preliminary indicators. Design and implementation of such systems involves numerous research challenges such as generic set of indicators, intelligence gathering, uncertainty reasoning and information fusion. This paper discusses such challenges and presents the reader with compelling motivation. A carefully deployed empirical analysis using a real world attack scenario and a real network traffic capture is also presented.

Keywords: Bayesian inference · Cyber defence · Cyber warfare · Future internet · Early warning systems

1 Introduction

Early warning systems for cyber defence is an emerging area of research which aims at alerting an attack attempt in its nascent stages. Wider definitions for a CEWS can be summarised as "a CEWS aims at detecting *unclassified* but potentially harmful system behaviour based on *preliminary indications* before possible damage occurs, and to *contribute* to an integrated and aggregated situation report" [1]. Although there can be many overlaps between a typical intrusion detection system (IDS) and a CEWS, a particular emphasis for a CEWS is to establish hypotheses and predictions as well as to generate advice on not yet understood (unclassified) situations based on preliminary indications [1]. In contrary, a typical IDS attempts to detect attack using *known indications of attack patterns* (these can be either signatures or anomalies) instead of using generic preliminary indications.

© IFIP International Federation for Information Processing
Published by Springer International Publishing Switzerland 2016. All Rights Reserved
J. Camenisch and D. Kesdoğan (Eds.): iNetSec 2015, LNCS 9591, pp. 29–42, 2016.
DOI: 10.1007/978-3-319-39028-4_3

This paper identifies some research challenges compounded by the nature of computing for design and implementation of effective CEWSs, and discusses potential solutions to overcome them. The paper starts with an empirical analysis in Sect. 2. Section 3 presents research challenges. Related work is presented in Sect. 4. Finally, Sect. 5 includes a discussion with necessary suggestions to move forward in this research line.

2   An Empirical Analysis

The sole purpose of this section is to demonstrate the feasibility of using preliminary indicators to produce early warnings in a situation when the known indicators of attack pattern is not available to use typical IDS techniques. This proof of principle case study built on an existing work [2].

2.1   Attack Scenario

We analyse the data set described in Sect. 2.2 for heartbleed exploits attempts. The heartbleed vulnerability [3] lies in the implementation of heartbeat protocol extension of the transport layer security (TLS). Heartbeat consists of two message types: heartbeat request and heartbeat response. When a request message received, the receiver must send a corresponding response message carrying an exact copy of the payload of the request by allocating a memory buffer as:

```
buffer = OPENSSL_malloc(1 + 2 + payload + padding)
```

There was no length check for this memory allocation in OpenSSL 1.0.1 and prior. Hence an attacker can specify higher payload values than the actual payload in the request and hence abuse the server to read arbitrary memory locations. This allows attackers to read sensitive memory (e.g. cryptographic keys and credentials) from vulnerable servers. Since there is a maximum boundary for the total length of a heartbeat message, in a heartbleed attack attempt, a higher number of message frequency can be expected during a connection in order to leak as much as possible data from the server's memory. It should be noted that it is necessary to look at and compare two fields k_1 and k_2 (see Table 1) in the TLS layer data to detect exploits attempts. If $k_1 > k_2$ then it is explicitly a heartbleed packet.

2.2   MAWI Data Set

In the MAWI data set, traffic traces have been collected during a 15 min period on each day at several sampling points within WIDE backbone - an operational testbed network in Japan [4]. After removing privacy information, traces have made open to the public. Hence traces consist of only protocol headers. Readers are invited to notice the limitations of details in the MAWI dataset with respect to heartbleed detection. Since TLS layer data is not available in the data set, it is not possible to explicitly check for heartbleed attack atempts. Therefore our aim is to analyse the dataset for the same attack scenario using a set of preliminary indicators as defined in Table 1.

Table 1. Two kind of indicators defined over a 443 session.

Known indicators to explicitly detect heartbleed exploit attempts by a typical IDS	Preliminary indicators to implicitly warn heartbleed exploit attempts by a CEWS
k_1 - requested payload length	i_1 - number of TCP segments from client to server
	i_2 - upload during a session
k_2 - actual payload length	i_3 - download during a session
	i_4 - time gap between two consecutive packets

2.3 Mathematical Basis

A node score is computed as follows. Let H be the hypothesis that given node (or IP address) is a heartbleed attacker and $I = \{i_1, i_2, i_3, i_4\}$ is a set of indicators defined within a 443 session (see Table 1). Assuming statistical independence between indicators and using well known log likelihood ratio,

$$ln\frac{P(H/I)}{P(\neg H/I)} = ln\frac{P(H)}{P(\neg H)} + \sum_k ln\frac{P(i_k/H)}{P(i_k/\neg H)} \tag{1}$$

During a smaller time window w, if $ln\frac{P(H/I)}{P(\neg H/I)} > 0$ then H is accepted. The rationale behind variable selection is that they are weakly connected to the behaviour of the heartbeat protocol. Our idea is to compare probability distributions of these variables in two populations, i.e. attack and clean, using Eq. 1. The prior belief $P(H)$ and $P(\neg H)$ were defined as follows.

$$p(H) = \begin{cases} 0.6, & \text{if the target node was doing a scan (port/host) prior to a session} \\ 0.4, & \text{otherwise} \end{cases} \tag{2}$$

The likelihood distributions $P(i_k/H)$ and $P(i_k/\neg H)$ were estimated using "malicious" and "clean" datasets respectively. Distribution for each variable were proposed by looking at their histograms. A dataset prior to December 2011 (i.e. before the bug was introduced in Open SSL) was chosen as the "clean" set. The "malicious" set was chosen based on our assumption that there is a higher chance for heartbleed attack attempt during the heartbleed public announcement period. This is due to practical constrains accessing for a sufficiently large known heartbleed dataset.

2.4 Experimental Setup and Outcomes

Fifteen minutes duration traces from each day was split into 90 segments, each segment is a 10 s window. Within a window, nodes are profiled using Eq. 1. If a node obtained negative $(-)$ scores throughout the observation period then that node is defined as "innocent". If a node obtained at least one positive $(+)$ score during the observation period then that node is defined as a "suspicious"

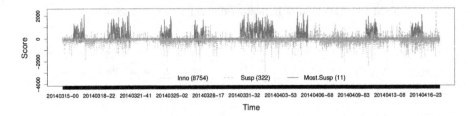

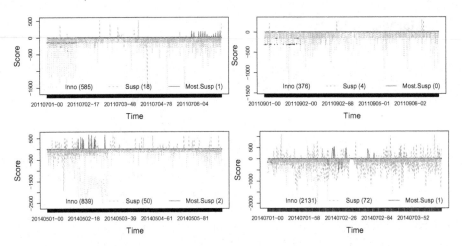

Fig. 1. Monitoring from 15.03.2014 to 16.04.2014 (during the heartbleed public announcement).

Fig. 2. Monitoring from July 2011 to July 2014 (selected graphs).

node. Among suspicious nodes, if any node stands out from their peer nodes (i.e. beyond three z-scores) then that node is identified as "most suspicious". Zero (0) means the target node has not produced any event that are of interest to this analysis during the observation window.

Figure 1 presents experimental outcome during heartbleed public announcement period. The graph presents the node score against the time line. Note that 11 and 322 nodes (out of 9087 nodes) were selected as most suspicious and suspicious nodes respectively in which proposed analysis has reduced the search space by 96%. In order to understand the recurrent of the target scenario by the same or different nodes, above analysis is repeated periodically (every two months) since July 2011 to July 2014. Due to the space constraint, only two graphs at the beginning and two graphs at the end of the analysis are presented in Fig. 2. A detailed description of the analysis can be found in our earlier paper [5].

Visual comparison between Figs. 1 and 2 gives an idea about the node behaviour over the period. Many nodes "stand out" from the normal behaviour during the heartbleed public announcement period in comparison to other periods. So, we would like to "early warn" about those nodes to carry out further investigations to classify their behaviour.

3   Research Challenges

Ability to early warn depends upon three factors: the progression rate of attack lifecycle (e.g. a malware propagation gives more early warning time than a typical denial of service (DOS) attack), amount of evidence left at each stage, and the ability to acquire such evidence by sensors. This section highlights few challenges associated with these factors.

3.1   Generic Set of Indicators

In other domains such as natural disasters (e.g. tsunami), kinetic warfare and medical diagnosis (e.g. diabetes) early warnings are well established, and arguably simple when compared to early warnings on the cyberspace. For example, in kinetic warfare, intelligence officers study different sources of intelligence (e.g. listen to communications, satellite imagery) to looking for known preliminary indicators of military mobilisation. In medical diagnosis, preliminary indicators such as feeling thirsty, tired, losing weight and blurred vision early warn an individual about diabetes. But on the cyberspace, it is not clear what these indicators are or how they can be observed [6]. This presents a huge problem when trying to develop CEWS. As many scholars argue [6,7], CEWS cannot be developed from a purely technical perspective. They must consider more than just technical indicators and require significant input from other disciplines such as international relations and sociology as the focus of CEWS should be to warn of an impending attack rather than detecting when it in progress. However the biggest challenge, a generic set of indicators (signs) of preparation for an attack on the cyberspace is not well established (understood) yet.

3.2   Intelligence Gathering

The cyberspace has a huge diversity. For example, it consists of different topological structures (e.g. PAN, LAN, MAN, WAN), different kind of networks (e.g. open Internet, darknet, honeynet, demilitarised zone) and different types of users (e.g. universities, health care system, the traffic system, power supply, trade, military networks). These entities produce events in different types and rates and have different analysis objectives and privacy requirements. In order to provide a representative image of the cyberspace at any given time, CEWS have to collect and process data from a range of these different entities. Employing a large monolithic sensor network for intelligence gathering on the cyberspace would not be possible due to these variations.

3.3   Uncertainty Reasoning

The cyberspace is an uncertain place. Hence cyber defenders have to deal with a great deal of uncertainty [8,9] which is compounded by the nature of computing. Any future CEWS that seeks to model and reasoning on the cyberspace has to accept this ground truth and must deal with incompleteness (compensate for lack of knowledge), inconsistencies (resolve ambiguities and contradictions) and change (update the knowledge base over time). For example, entering misspelled password can be a simple mistake by an innocent user or a password guessing attempt by an attacker. Cyber defenders do not know who the attackers nor their location. Some suspicious events, e.g. a major router failure could generate many ICMP unreachable messages while some computer worms (e.g. CodeRed and Nimda) generate the same in active probing process, can appear as part of an attack as well as can originate from normal network activities. Other contextual information should be utilised to narrow down the meaning of such data [8].

3.4   Scalability

In principal it is possible to log every activity on every device on the cyberspace, but in practice security analysts cannot process these logs due to their vagueness as attack indicators as well as the sheer volume of data. The biggest challenge is how to start from imprecise and limited knowledge about attack possibilities, and quickly sift through huge volume of data to spot a small set of data that altogether makes the picture of attacks clear. As volume and rate of traffic are rising, inspection of each and every individual event is not feasible. A data reduction is needed [8].

3.5   Information Fusion

As mentioned earlier, CEWS cannot be developed from a purely technical perspective. Given the huge number of possible data sources and overwhelming amount of data they generate, a data reduction method is essential to enable continuous security monitoring [10]. Future CEWS require fusing as many data sources as possible. Though it is not an exhaustive list some possible data sources for this task would be network data traffic, log files, social media, mobile location traces, mobile call traffic, web browsing traces, content popularity, user preferences, spatial/geographic distribution of network elements, network topology (router and AS level), network paths, protocol traces, social network structure and other security intelligence either system or social level.

3.6   Evaluation

Getting validity for a novel method is only possible through a proper evaluation. But in this research area, evaluation of novel algorithms against real time network data is a challenge. Real network traffic datasets with ground truth data on attack activity are difficult to obtain. Any such effort faces uncertainty of success in investigating relevant patterns of activity. One solution to this problem would be to develop monitoring algorithms based on unary classification as it is relatively easier to find clean datasets than malicious ones, or providing mathematical proof for novel methods.

4   Related Work

This section provides an overview of the existing practices for CEWS and provides a brief evaluation of some significant ideas to give future directions. Design and implementation of effective CEWS has a significant amount of overlaps with other research areas [6] such as situational awareness, intrusion detection and network monitoring. Hence we categorise them in related themes.

4.1   Threat Scenario

Threat scenario provides an important aspect to the early warning discussion. For example, early warning on malware propagation can be easier than warning on DOS attack. The former needs a period of time to propagate and hence provides long early warning time (typically minutes to days). However early warning on DOS can be problematic as it might last within few seconds. Attempts to early warn on a particular threat type is common (e.g. [11–15]) in the literature. A malware warning centre is proposed in [11] which uses a Kalman filter to detect a worm's propagation at its early stage in real-time. An architecture of an automatic CEWS is discussed in [12]. Authors aim to provide predictions and advice regarding security threats without incorporation of cognitive abilities of humans. [13] aims for distributed, large-scale monitoring of malware on the Internet. A worm propagation stochastic model is built [14] to model the random effects during worm spreading by means of a stochastic differential equation. Authors propose a logical framework for a distributed early warning system against unknown and fast-spreading worms. An open-source early warning system to estimate the threat level and the malicious activities across the Internet is provided [15]. Limiting to a certain threat type is a major drawback of above proposals. They cannot simply extend for newly emerging threats.

4.2   Situational Awareness

Situational awareness is an essential component of an CEWS, and hence related to this work. Cyber situational awareness includes awareness of suspicious network related activities that can take place at all levels in the TCP/IP stack [16]. Such activity can range from low-level network sniffing to suspicious linguistic content on social media. Various network measurements and techniques (e.g. packet inter arrival times [17], deep packet inspection [18], game theory [19]) have been employed in proposing these solutions. The idea for a common operational picture (big picture) is presented [20,21]. A systematic review of cyber situational awareness can be found in [16]. However instead of addressing the full complexity, above solutions concentrated on a particular issue of the problem and some solutions (e.g. deep packet inspection) are neither feasible in practice nor suitable for real time analysis.

4.3   Information Exchange

DShield internet storm centre is a cooperative network security community. It collects firewall and IDS logs world wide and incorporates human interpretation and action in order to generate predictions and advice [22]. eCSIRT.net [23] comprises of a sensor network which collects and correlates alerts for human inspection. The Internet motion sensor, a globally scoped Internet monitoring system aims to measure, characterise, and track threats [24]. It statistically analyses dark net traffic that needs to be interpreted by humans. DeepSight intelligence collects, analyses and delivers cyber-threat information through a editable portal and datafeeds, enabling proactive defensive actions and improved incident response [25]. Human analysis and data mining is incorporated in order to provide statistics. An infrastructure and organisational framework for a situation awareness and early warning system for the Internet is presented in [26]. This work aims for sharing, correlating and cooperatively analysing sensor data collected from number of organisations located in different geographical locations. eDare (Early Detection, Alert and Response system) [27] and the Agent-based CEWS [28] also focus on early warning in computer networks. However information exchange can be seen as a major barrier for CEWS' advances. In the context of security, data and information sharing is difficult between different organisations and nations due to various reasons [29, 30]. An extensive survey of collaborative intrusion detection proposals can be found in [22].

4.4   Sensor Networks

Sensing in-progress attacks requires strategically placed sensors throughout the cyberspace, and analysing acquired data to distinguish between attack traffic (events) and innocent traffic. Sensor network would be a vital part of CEWS. Current sensor networks for CEWS have a simple monolithic structure [31], where data is acquired at the network edges and then transmitted over a dumb infrastructure to a central location for analysis. This can cause various issues to the analysis due to many reasons such as nonidentical measurements, nonidentical local detectors and noisy channels [32]. High computational cost is another significant issue. Hence computationally fast and accurate methodology to evaluate the error, detection, and false alarm probabilities in such networks is essential. Optimal sensor placement strategies for CEWS is discussed in [33]. Authors study correlation between attack patterns of different locations (national and international) and explore how sensors should be located accordingly. The design and analysis of sensor networks for detection applications has received considerable attention during past decades [34].

4.5   Information Fusion

Technical data itself is not sufficient to produce early warnings on computer networks. Fusion of different network measurements from different sources is essential. That measurement could be range from low-level network sniffing to suspicious linguistic contents on social media. A number of techniques have been employed last decades for information fusion on computer networks. Fusion of cyber-related information from a variety of resources including commercial news, blogs, wikis, and social media sources is proposed in [35]. Bayesian fusion for slow activity monitoring [8,36], high speed information fusion for real-time situational awareness [37], JDL data fusion model to computer networks [38], detecting network data patterns [39], combining data from sensors using ontology methods [40] and fuse security audit data with data from a psychological model [41] are few of them to mention. Using web-based text as a source for identifying emerging and ongoing attacks can be found in [42].

4.6   Tools and Techniques

Most existing tools and techniques have been dedicated for security data analytic. An open, adaptable, and extensible visual analytic framework is provided in [43]. All data is treated as streaming and visualises them using machine learning techniques [44], live network situational awareness system that relies upon streaming algorithms included [45], fast calculations of important statistical properties of high speed and high volume data [45], sophisticated visualization of attack paths and automatic recommendations for mitigation [46] are some interesting works in the literature. In this context, there is a need to investigate "changes to the changing patterns" instead of changing points in a traffic profile sequence. This is essential as there are general systematic patterns (e.g. trend and seasonality) in the time series of user behaviours, and such variations should be considered as pretty normal in the analysis. Autocorrelations and differencing could help to deal with general dependencies in the data to make hidden patterns apparent and relevant.

5   Discussion

Instead of addressing the full complexity, existing works are concentrated on particular cyber issues such as sensor placement, type of sensors, data fusion and packet sampling. In order to deal with toady's advanced threats, an integrated large scale security analytic is needed. These advanced threats are the work of hacktivists, nation states, criminal enterprises and other groups with deep funding and specialised security expertise. They conduct reconnaissance not only on an organisation's security systems but also personnel and processes, and develop techniques to exploit them through social engineering, escalation of privileges and other forms of probing attacks. They move patiently through an organisation's network - taking days, weeks or months to accomplish their objectives - in order to avoid detection [47]. In principal, early warning on such attacks is feasible as they provide long early warning time, but in practice research challenges discussed in the paper has to overcome to design and implement such a system.

As discussed in Sect. 3.1 establishing a generic set of indicators is the biggest challenge. In empirical analysis in Sect. 2, preliminary indicators defined using the existing knowledge of heartbleed attack. But how to derive a set of preliminary indicators for zero day attacks? One possible approach to address this would be building a complete (as much as possible) corpus of recently discovered attacks such as Stuxnet, Duqu 2.0 and Havex, and analysing that corpus in order to derive a generic set of indicators. This analysis should focus on each stage of attack lifecycle (e.g. reconnaissance, inspection paths, lateral movements, data ex-filtration and C2 activities) of each attack in the corpus.

Monolithic sensor network for intelligence gathering would not be suitable beyond research test beds. Deploying sensor networks with huge variations in administrative distribution and cooperation are required for advances in future CEWS. Investigations on how ordinary sensors can be employed to handle these type of complexities has not been covered much in the literature. Investigations to improve some exiting works (e.g. [32]) to fit this purpose would be interesting.

As discussed in Sect. 3.3, not modelling the uncertainty in event classification is a major issue in many existing IDSs. As a result they produce huge number of false alarms, in which existing security monitoring tools bring significant amount of uncertainty to the true interpretation of security alerts. The uncertainty challenge exists in all stages of generic attack process [48]. There are three basics methods that can be employed to handle these kind of uncertainties: symbolic methods, statistical techniques and fuzzy methods. Efficient methods needed to leverage advances in these methods and other system level techniques for early estimation of malicious activities.

Applying a data reduction technique would be possible method to address scalability issues. Employing statistical sampling [8,49] and/or suitable approximation techniques (e.g. approximate Bayesian computation, saddle point approximation) would be possible methods to reduce the computational cost involved in the analysis. Node profiling through information fusion may address some issues such as storage [8]. Low-rank approximation [50] in minimisation problem in mathematical modelling and data compression would be interesting to investigate as a data reduction method on the cyberspace. Such a work can be found in [51].

As mentioned in Sect. 3.5, analysing a centralised log collection or traffic capture is not longer enough for modern day security. While probabilistic fusion may be useful, a systematic investigation still needs to evaluate approaches for the ability to handle vagueness (fuzzy set), ambiguity (dempster-shafer) and incompleteness (possibilistic) of events, ultimately with an aim to develop hybrid data fusion techniques useful for early estimation. Events in the physical world offer additional sensors providing insight regarding the on going situation. Recent developments using Bayesian-based statistical profiling of potential targets of cyber attacks provides for a promise to address this as it accommodates for analyst's prior belief [52,53].

References

1. Biskup, J., Hämmerli, B., Meier, M., Schmerl, S., Tölle, J., Vogel, M.: 2. 08102 working group-early warning systems. In: Proceedings biskup_et_al: DSP, 1493 (2008)
2. Lee, C., Yi, L., Tan, L.H., Goh, W., Lee, B.S., Yeo, C.K.: A wavelet entropy-based change point detection on network traffic: a case study of heartbleed vulnerability. In: 2014 IEEE 6th International Conference on Cloud Computing Technology and Science (CloudCom), pp. 995–1000, December 2014
3. Durumeric, Z., Kasten, J., Adrian, D., Halderman, J.A., Bailey, M., Li, F., Weaver, N., Amann, J., Beekman, J., Payer, M., et al.: The matter of heartbleed. In: Proceedings of the 2014 Conference on Internet Measurement Conference, pp. 475–488. ACM (2014)
4. Cho, K., Mitsuya, K., Kato, A.: Traffic data repository at the wide project. In: Proceedings of the Annual Conference on USENIX Annual Technical Conference, ATEC 2000, p. 51. USENIX Association, Berkeley (2000)
5. Kalutarage, H., Shaikh, S., Lee, C., Sung, F.: Towards an early warning system for network attacks using bayesian inference. In: 2015 IEEE 2nd International Conference on Cyber Security and Cloud Computing (CSCloud), pp. 399–404, November 2015
6. Robinson, M., Jones, K., Janicke, H.: Cyber warfare: issues and challenges. Comput. Secur. **49**, 70–94 (2015)
7. Sharma, A., Gandhi, R., Mahoney, W., Sousan, W., Zhu, Q., et al.: Building a social dimensional threat model from current and historic events of cyber attacks. In: 2010 IEEE Second International Conference on Social Computing (SocialCom), pp. 981–986. IEEE (2010)
8. Kalutarage, H.K., Shaikh, S.A., Wickramasinghe, I.P., Zhou, Q., James, A.E.: Detecting stealthy attacks: efficient monitoring of suspicious activities on computer networks. Comput. Electr. Eng. **47**, 327–344 (2015)
9. Kalutarage, H.: Effective monitoring of slow suspicious activites on computer networks. Ph.D. thesis, Coventry University (2013)
10. Dempsey, K.: Information security continuous monitoring (ISCM) for federal information systems and organizations. US Department of Commerce, National Institute of Standards and Technology (2011)
11. Zou, C.C., Gao, L., Gong, W., Towsley, D.: Monitoring and early warning for internet worms. In: Proceedings of the 10th ACM Conference on Computer and Communications Security, pp. 190–199. ACM (2003)
12. Apel, M., Biskup, J., Flegel, U., Meier, M.: Towards early warning systems – challenges, technologies and architecture. In: Rome, E., Bloomfield, R. (eds.) CRITIS 2009. LNCS, vol. 6027, pp. 151–164. Springer, Heidelberg (2010)
13. Engelberth, M., Freiling, F.C., Göbel, J., Gorecki, C., Holz, T., Hund, R., Trinius, P., Willems, C.: The inmas approach (2010)
14. Magkos, E., Avlonitis, M., Kotzanikolaou, P., Stefanidakis, M.: Toward early warning against internet worms based on critical-sized networks. Secur. Commun. Netw. **6**(1), 78–88 (2013)
15. Kollias, S., Vlachos, V., Papanikolaou, A., Chatzimisios, P., Ilioudis, C., Metaxiotis, K.: Measuring the internet's threat level: a global-local approach. In: 2014 IEEE Symposium on Computers and Communication (ISCC), pp. 1–6. IEEE (2014)
16. Franke, U., Brynielsson, J.: Cyber situational awareness-a systematic review of the literature. Comput. Secur. **46**, 18–31 (2014)

17. Harmer, P., Thomas, R., Christel, B., Martin, R., Watson, C.: Wireless security situation awareness with attack identification decision support. In: 2011 IEEE Symposium on Computational Intelligence in Cyber Security (CICS), pp. 144–151, April 2011

18. King, D., Orlando, G., Kohler, J.: A case for trusted sensors: encryptors with deep packet inspection capabilities. In: Military Communication Conference, MILCOM 2012, pp. 1–6. IEEE (2012)

19. He, H., Xiaojing, W., Xin, Y.: A decision-support model for information systems based on situational awareness. In: International Conference on Multimedia Information Networking and Security, MINES 2009, vol. 2, pp. 405–408, November 2009

20. Cheng, Y., Sagduyu, Y., Deng, J., Li, J., Liu, P.: Integrated situational awareness for cyber attack detection, analysis, and mitigation. In: SPIE Defense, Security, and Sensing, International Society for Optics and Photonics, p. 83850N (2012)

21. Preden, J., Motus, L., Meriste, M., Riid, A.: Situation awareness for networked systems. In: 2011 IEEE First International Multi-Disciplinary Conference on Cognitive Methods in Situation Awareness and Decision Support (CogSIMA), pp. 123–130, February 2011

22. Zhou, C.V., Leckie, C., Karunasekera, S.: A survey of coordinated attacks and collaborative intrusion detection. Comput. Secur. **29**(1), 124–140 (2010)

23. CSIRT_Network: The european computer security incident response team network, June 2015. http://www.ecsirt.net/

24. Bailey, M., Cooke, E., Jahanian, F., Nazario, J., Watson, D., et al.: The internet motion sensor-a distributed blackhole monitoring system. In: NDSS (2005)

25. Symantec: Cyber security: Deepsight intelligence, June 2015. http://www.symantec.com/deepsight-products/

26. Grobauer, B., Mehlau, J.I., Sander, J.: Carmentis: a co-operative approach towards situation awareness and early warning for the internet. In: IMF, pp. 55–66 (2006)

27. Elovici, Y., Shabtai, A., Moskovitch, R., Tahan, G., Glezer, C.: Applying machine learning techniques for detection of malicious code in network traffic. In: Hertzberg, J., Beetz, M., Englert, R. (eds.) KI 2007. LNCS (LNAI), vol. 4667, pp. 44–50. Springer, Heidelberg (2007)

28. Bsufka, K., Kroll-Peters, O., Albayrak, Ş.: Intelligent network-based early warning systems. In: López, J. (ed.) CRITIS 2006. LNCS, vol. 4347, pp. 103–111. Springer, Heidelberg (2006)

29. Brunner, M., Hofinger, H., Roblee, C., Schoo, P., Todt, S.: Anonymity and privacy in distributed early warning systems. In: Xenakis, C., Wolthusen, S. (eds.) CRITIS 2010. LNCS, vol. 6712, pp. 81–92. Springer, Heidelberg (2011)

30. Koch, R., Golling, M., Rodosek, G.D.: Evaluation of state of the art ids message exchange protocols. In: International Conference on Communication and Network Security (ICCNS) (2013)

31. Theilmann, A.: Beyond centralism: the herold approach to sensor networks and early warning systems. In: Proceedings of First European Workshop of Internet Early Warning and Network Intelligence (EWNI 2010) (2010)

32. Aldosari, S., Moura, J.M., et al.: Detection in sensor networks: the saddlepoint approximation. IEEE Trans. Sig. Process. **55**(1), 327–340 (2007)

33. Göbel, J., Trinius, P.: Towards optimal sensor placement strategies for early warning systems. In: Sicherheit, pp. 191–204 (2010)

34. Varshney, P.K.: Distributed Detection and Data Fusion. Springer Science & Business Media, New York (1997)

35. Morris, T., Mayron, L., Smith, W., Knepper, M., Ita, R., Fox, K.: A perceptually-relevant model-based cyber threat prediction method for enterprise mission assurance. In: 2011 IEEE First International Multi-Disciplinary Conference on Cognitive Methods in Situation Awareness and Decision Support (CogSIMA), pp. 60–65, February 2011

36. Chivers, H., Clark, J.A., Nobles, P., Shaikh, S.A., Chen, H.: Knowing who to watch: identifying attackers whose actions are hidden within false alarms and background noise. Inf. Syst. Front. **15**(1), 17–34 (2013)

37. Sudit, M., Stotz, A., Holender, M.: Situational awareness of a coordinated cyber attack. In: Defense and Security, International Society for Optics and Photonics, pp. 114–129 (2005)

38. Schreiber-Ehle, S., Koch, W.: The jdl model of data fusion applied x2014; a review paper. In: 2012 Workshop on Sensor Data Fusion: Trends, Solutions, Applications (SDF), pp. 116–119, September 2012

39. Paffenroth, R., Du Toit, P., Nong, R., Scharf, L., Jayasumana, A.P., Bandara, V.: Space-time signal processing for distributed pattern detection in sensor networks. IEEE J. Sel. Top. Sig. Proces. **7**(1), 38–49 (2013)

40. Mathews, M.L., Halvorsen, P., Joshi, A., Finin, T.: A collaborative approach to situational awareness for cybersecurity. In: 2012 8th International Conference on Collaborative Computing: Networking, Applications and Worksharing (CollaborateCom), pp. 216–222. IEEE (2012)

41. Greitzer, F.L., Frincke, D.A.: Combining traditional cyber security audit data with psychosocial data: towards predictive modeling for insider threat mitigation. In: Probst, C.W., et al. (eds.) Insider Threats in Cyber Security, pp. 85–113. Springer, New York (2010)

42. Grothoff, K., Brunner, M., Hofinger, H., Roblee, C., Eckert, C.: Problems in web-based open source information processing for it early warning (2011)

43. Jonker, D., Langevin, S., Schretlen, P., Canfield, C.: Agile visual analytics for banking cyber x201c;big data x201d;. In: 2012 IEEE Conference on Visual Analytics Science and Technology (VAST), pp. 299–300, October 2012

44. Harrison, L., Laska, J., Spahn, R., Iannacone, M., Downing, E., Ferragut, E.M., Goodall, J.R.: situ: Situational understanding and discovery for cyber attacks. In: 2012 IEEE Conference on Visual Analytics Science and Technology (VAST), pp. 307–308, October 2012

45. Streilein, W.W., Truelove, J., Meiners, C.R., Eakman, G.: Cyber situational awareness through operational streaming analysis. In: Military Communications Conference, MILCOM 2011, pp. 1152–1157. IEEE (2011)

46. Jajodia, S., Noel, S., Kalapa, P., Albanese, M., Williams, J.: Cauldron mission-centric cyber situational awareness with defense in depth. In: Military Communications Conference, MILCOM 2011, pp. 1339–1344. IEEE (2011)

47. Weber, D.: Transforming traditional security strategies into an early warning system for advanced threats, September 2012. http://www.emc.com/collateral/software/solution-overview/h11031-transforming-traditional-security-strategies-so.pdf

48. Li, J., Ou, X., Rajagopalan, R.: Uncertainty and risk management in cyber situational awareness. In: Jajodia, S., et al. (eds.) Cyber Situational Awareness, pp. 51–68. Springer, New York (2010)

49. Kalutarage, H.K., Shaikh, S.A., Zhou, Q., James, A.E.: Monitoring for slow suspicious activities using a target centric approach. In: Bagchi, A., Ray, I. (eds.) ICISS 2013. LNCS, vol. 8303, pp. 163–168. Springer, Heidelberg (2013)

50. Markovsky, I.: Low Rank Approximation: Algorithms, Implementation, Applications. Springer Science & Business Media, New York (2011)

51. Viswanath, B., Bashir, M.A., Crovella, M., Guha, S., Gummadi, K.P., Krishnamurthy, B., Mislove, A.: Towards detecting anomalous user behavior in online social networks. In: Proceedings of the 23rd USENIX Security Symposium (USENIX Security) (2014)

52. Kalutarage, H.K., Shaikh, S.A., Zhou, Q., James, A.E.: Sensing for suspicion at scale: a bayesian approach for cyber conflict attribution and reasoning. In: 2012 4th International Conference on Cyber Conflict (CYCON), pp. 1–19. IEEE (2012)

53. Shaikh, S.A., Kalutarage, H.K.: Effective network security monitoring: from attribution to target-centric monitoring. Telecommun. Syst. **62**, 167–178 (2015)

Catching Inside Attackers: Balancing Forensic Detectability and Privacy of Employees

Ephraim Zimmer[(✉)], Jens Lindemann, Dominik Herrmann,
and Hannes Federrath

Computer Science Department, University of Hamburg, Hamburg, Germany
{ephraim.zimmer,jens.lindemann,dominik.herrmann,
hannes.federrath}@informatik.uni-hamburg.de

Abstract. IT departments of organisations go to great lengths to protect their IT infrastructure from external attackers. However, internal attacks also pose a large threat to organisations. Despite detection and prevention of insider attacks being an active field of research, so far such techniques are rarely being deployed in practice. This paper outlines the state of the art in the field and identifies open research problems in the area. The lack of unified definitions and publicly available datasets for evaluation is detrimental to the comparability of published results in the field and hinders the continual improvement of technology. Another important problem is that of data protection: On the one hand, the data captured for insider attack detection could also be used for surveillance of employees, so it should be anonymised. On the other hand, anonymisation may make some attacks undetectable, leading to a trade-off between detectability of attacks and privacy.

1 Introduction

Nowadays, an organisation's IT infrastructure will typically be connected to the Internet. Internal and external communications rely on digital technology and employees often require the Internet to research information necessary for their day-to-day work. To protect against attacks from the Internet, which have increased dramatically in recent years [3], IT security departments rely on established security mechanisms, such as firewalls, Intrusion Detection Systems (IDS), honeypots and so-called De-Militarised Zones (DMZ). These measures are intended to stop external attackers who are trying to interfere with the execution of business processes or obtain internal assets, such as trade secrets or confidential customer data. However, the danger arising from attacks originating from within the organisation itself is often overlooked.

A workshop on *Countering Insider Threads* in 2008 defined an *inside attacker* as "a person that has been legitimately empowered with the right to access, represent, or decide about one or more assets of the organization's structure" [26]. However, the term is not defined consistently throughout the scientific literature. According to Pfleeger, an inside attacker can also be "anyone properly identified and authenticated to the system including, perhaps, someone masquerading as a

© IFIP International Federation for Information Processing
Published by Springer International Publishing Switzerland 2016. All Rights Reserved
J. Camenisch and D. Kesdoğan (Eds.): iNetSec 2015, LNCS 9591, pp. 43–55, 2016.
DOI: 10.1007/978-3-319-39028-4_4

legitimate insider, or someone to whom an insider has given access (for example by sharing a password)" [25]. The two examples include regular employees as well as sophisticated system administrators, but give different context variabilities of an inside attacker. The former implicitly exclude outside attackers masquerading as insiders, whereas the latter includes those scenarios into its definition.

Insider attacks are a major threat for organisations. As insiders typically have extensive access rights (especially if they are system administrators) and possess detailed knowledge about the IT infrastructure of their organisation, they know where to strike for maximum impact and are capable of hiding their activities. In a survey of the CERT Insider Threat Center among US companies 47 percent of companies acknowledged that they were knowingly affected by insider attacks throughout the years 2004 to 2013 [5]. The dark figure might very well exceed this number significantly, as insider attacks often are either not detected by organisations or withheld from the public due to the high risk of reputation loss. Less than half of those surveyed companies have deployed defined mechanisms and procedures to deal with insider attacks [23]. Experts estimate the impact of insider attacks on the German economy at about 50 billion Euros per year [32].

The security mechanisms that are currently in practical use cannot adequately detect attacks by insiders. Due to their access rights and inside knowledge, insiders can hide malicious activity significantly easier than external attackers, e. g. by deactivating security systems or manipulating log files. Moreover, insider attacks are hard to detect at the network perimeter, where traditional security mechanisms are typically located.

Even though several technical detection and prevention mechanisms have been proposed by various researchers, those mechanisms have not reached widespread practical implementation and deployment yet. Currently, insider threats are mainly being countered by organisational measures, such as by imposing a two-man rule for actions having a high impact on security (e. g. disabling a firewall or modifying log files) [4,30].

In discussions about insider attack detection, data protection is often overlooked. However, comprehensive logs for detecting and attributing insider attacks can reveal a lot of information about the behaviour of employees, thereby invading their privacy. On the other hand, if too much anonymisation is performed before passing the data to a detection algorithm, some attacks may not be detectable anymore.

The remainder of the paper is structured as follows. In Sect. 2, we describe the state of the art in detection and prevention mechanisms for insider attacks. Section 3 shows some avenues for future research. In Sect. 4, challenges for the development of the field are presented, before the paper is concluded in Sect. 5.

2   State of the Art in Detection and Prevention Mechanisms

Researchers have proposed to counter insider threats by means of technical and non-technical mechanisms [9,27]. With the help of technical solutions, attack detection and monitoring data can be collected, correlated and analysed for insider activities during or after an insider attack. Non-technical solutions and best practices serve the goal of insider detection and prevention by providing strict policies and evaluating information about social behaviour, an employee's productivity or insights from Human Resources (HR), like imminent employee terminations. (Semi-)automatic collection and assessment of this kind of data as well as the establishment of corporation-wide guidelines, employee training and formal policies (focussing on insider threats) are supposed to effectively unveil and eliminate insider activities and attacks. In the following, we review recent insider threat research and related work.

2.1   Non-technical Means of Protection

In terms of organisational or structural protection mechanisms against the insider threat, the literature focuses mainly on motivation- and opportunity-based countermeasures. Examples are the destruction of incentives for insider attacks [24], training to change employees' mindsets as well as a close cooperation with HR to obtain deep insight into employees' projects and groups to identify employees who need to have access to sensitive data [14].

Silowash et al. [30] took a more structured approach and developed a common sense guide to mitigating insider threads including various practices to prepare an organisation for correctly dealing with insider threats. Among those practices, the guide considers the following non-technical countermeasures:

- Consider threats from insiders and business partners in enterprise-wide risk assessments.
- Clearly document and consistently enforce policies and controls.
- Incorporate insider threat awareness into periodic security training for all employees.
- Beginning with the hiring process, monitor and respond to suspicious or disruptive behaviour.
- Anticipate and manage negative issues in the work environment.
- Know your assets.
- Enforce separation of duties and least privilege.
- Develop a comprehensive employee termination procedure.
- Develop a formalised insider threat program.

This guide as well as other proposed non-technical countermeasures are mainly derived from control domains specified in Annex A of ISO 27001, as Coles-Kemp and Theoharidou showed [6], and deal with the insider threat on a very high and abstract level. It takes a lot of effort and the involvement of a whole corporation to realise and run them in practice. Furthermore, due to the corporation-specific execution of practices it is difficult to transfer them to another corporation or environment.

2.2   Technical Means of Protection

At first sight, most, if not all, traditional technical countermeasures that are used to protect organisations against cyber attacks (like Intrusion Detection Systems (IDSs) and log data analysis) may also be employed to detect and prevent insider activites. However, the domain and circumstances of an insider attack are fundamentally different: On the one hand, this leads to significantly more alerts and increased false positive rates. On the other hand, those mechanisms might possibly be tricked or circumvented by insiders with the help of their specific and internal knowledge.

Behavioural Profiling of Users. Research on technical protection mechanisms against insider attacks has devoted a lot of attention to profiling employee behaviour. Here, the objective is to learn the legitimate characteristics of users in order to perform (semi-)automatic detection of potentially anomalous insider activities. These approaches also strike the threat of masqueraders, who are outside attackers possessing stolen credentials of employees and therefore have access to inside resources and systems.

Schonlau et al. [28] studied possibilities of detecting insider attacks by profiling Unix shell commands. Over several months, they collected shell commands of 50 different users and additionally simulated insider activities by injecting commands of users who played the role of masqueraders. Based on this dataset, they tried to evaluate different methods of anomaly detection. The results showed a rather high rate of false alarms as well as false negatives. Later, other researchers re-used the Schonlau dataset, applying improved detection methods [21]. Although promising, the Schonlau dataset does not provide a very good base for evaluating insider attack detection mechanisms as the masquerader simulation is rather artificial and Unix is only a small part of employees' production environments.

Other approaches considered user profiling in the context of the graphical user interface of Microsoft Windows. Goldring [10] evaluated user profiling by periodically collecting data from the Windows process table in short intervals. This data shows the lifecycle and additional information (such as owner and CPU usage) of all programs that have been or are running on a system. To filter out operating system noise, Goldring exploited the fact that each user interaction with the system takes place in a window. Therefore, he additionally took window titles into account. The resulting concept looks promising, but associated evaluation results have not been published.

Li and Manicopoulos [17] also studied profiling of Windows users. They created a dataset with simulated insider attacks (similar to the Schonlau dataset) and applied a one-class Support Vector Machine (SVM) to build models of legitimate user behaviours. With this model, a binary classifier could be used to test new models for compliance or deviation. However, their technique achieves only moderate accuracy in terms of detection and false alarms rates and their dataset entails the same deficiencies as the Schonlau dataset.

Network-Based Approaches. Besides host-based user behaviour profiling, corporate network traffic comprises a great source of information about employees' IT activities and thus valuable data for insider attack detection and prevention mechanisms. Spitzner [31] applied the now widespread knowledge and application of honeypots and honeytokens from the domain of outsider attack countermeasures and perimeter threats to the insider threat. The idea is to stimulate the interest of inside attackers, who are looking for some kind of valuable information, in specialised honeytokens. Whenever attackers access a honeytoken, they are automatically redirected to a honeypot, where the interaction can be monitored and analysed in a secure environment. Although interesting as a means to decrease false positive rates in insider detection mechanisms, the concept has not been evaluated, which by design is very hard to conduct. Only empirical evaluation of practically deployed systems could provide reliable results, as simulated insider attacks are not suitable. Further, the effectiveness of honeytokens and honeypots in insider attack detection and prevention is highly dependent on several attributes of an inside attacker, like knowledge of countermeasures, technical skill level and level of suspicion.

Maloof and Stephens [20] also concentrated their work on network traffic collection and analysis. They created a system called ELICIT, which aims at the detection of inside attackers, who try to access information they do not need to know according to their job description and similar additionally acquired information. The ELICIT system consists of four parts: First, network traffic is collected and prepared in the form of events. Secondly, events are enriched with additional contextual information about employees and alerts are issued. Thirdly, a threat score is calculated based on a Bayesian network, which takes these alerts as input. Finally, the scores are presented for further examination by security personnel. The authors evaluated their system by collecting internal data of an organisation over several months, replayed activities from publicly known past insider attack cases and applied the dataset offline to ELICIT afterwards. The evaluation showed very good results in terms of detection rates and remarkably low false positive rates. However, the system strongly relies on the presence of machine-interpretable contextual information about employees, job descriptions, need-to-know domains and such. For this information to be present, a corporation needs to have strict HR policies and comprehensive procedures in place, which may hinder adoption in practice. Additionally, the simulated execution of past insider attacks occurred over few days in contrast to real world insider attacks, which more likely occur over several weeks, months or years [27].

2.3   Integrated Approaches

Recent proposals go one step further and try to integrate non-technical approaches with technical countermeasures to combine their advantages and create comprehensive insider attack detection and especially prevention systems. Greitzer and Frincke [12] took psychological data in addition to classical security audit data into account. The objective was to create possibilities in predicting insider activities of employees by means of a set of predictive indicators and an integration and analysis framework for organisational, social and cyber security data. Costa et al. [7] created an ontology-based approach by studying 800 real-world insider attack cases, allowing them to identify entities involved, insider actions conducted, assets targeted and events triggered. This information was translated into an insider threat indicator ontology and combined and enriched with (semi-)automatically processable operational context data from HR. With the help of a semantic reasoner, which monitors current activities and responsibilities of a corporation and evaluates this information against the ontology, potential insider activities could be identified and alerted.

Major challenges for all integrated approaches were found to be the lack of reliable testing and evaluation datasets, no operational evaluation, privacy and ethical issues, and the need for extensive training and awareness of employees.

3　Avenues for Future Research

The measures outlined in the previous Section aim to effectively detect or prevent insider attacks. However, these measures ignore some fundamental problems, which will be outlined in the following.

3.1　Unified Definition of Terms, Motives and Tools

Research on insider attacks is only meaningful in the context of a concrete adversary model that describes capabilities and motives. For instance, system administrators are more powerful than regular employees due to their extensive access to all IT infrastructure and monitoring devices. Moreover, strategically-acting intentional attackers have to be treated differently than users who bring their own devices to work and infect the corporate network with malware inadvertently. With modern forms of e-commerce and outsourcing of IT services, even third parties may act like insiders [13]. Customers who rent infrastracture or software as a service can either interfere with the underlying infrastructure or exploit it to launch attacks against others [18].

Despite experts from science, industry, the financial sector, and the US government concluding that there is a lack of standardised definitions for insiders and insider attacks during a workshop on *Insider Attack and Cyber Security* in 2007 [25], there are still no such definitions. This leads to scientists using different definitions for their research, typically choosing a definition that is beneficial to their research project and expected outcome. As already stated with the two examples of a definition in Sect. 1, different foci on the context variabilities of an inside attacker for example provide different, sometimes even competing results. This leads to a delusive comparison of countermeasures, which seem to provide solutions for the same insider problem, when in fact the problem domain is significantly different. Even four years later, scientists aiming to establish unified definitions came to the conclusion that additional, more detailed definitions would have to be established [13]. The authors state, that current definitions lack the reflection of two recent developments. First, the new capabilities and applications of networked environments. And second, the increasingly indistinct separation of corporation boundaries. Further, the characterisation of inside attackers becomes progressively multidimensional, emphasising different capabilities or circumstances of an inside attacker or an insider attack.

As a conclusion, this leads to diverging results being published by different research groups on the one hand. On the other hand, the comparability of published results is impeded by the lack of unified definitions, which leads to continuous improvement of scientific results not taking place.

3.2 Generation of Datasets

Technical approaches for detection and prevention of insider attacks published by scientists – such as [7] – have so far failed to find widespread use in practice [27]. This can partly be attributed to the unsatisfactory effectiveness of these approaches, as is evident by their high false positive and false negative rates. Another problem is that it is difficult for researchers to evaluate their proposed solutions in a way that approximates their behaviour in a real production environment and allows a comparison between results published by different research groups. This is due to the lack of comprehensive datasets of insider attacks captured in a real production environment, which could be used for realistically evaluating effectiveness and efficiency [13, 27]. Existing datasets have either been taken from a different context (e. g. the Schonlau dataset [28]) or have been derived from simulations that made special assumptions about the attacking insider and the organisation (such as time restrictions or existing formal regulations [20]). As these methods for generating datasets cannot provide a realistic approximation of insider attacks [27], they are not useful for evaluating detection mechanisms.

3.3 Software Implementations and Their Evaluation

Software implementations of scientifically proposed solutions for the detection and prevention of insider attacks as well as the (semi-)automatic collection and evaluation of additional information sources – as proposed by Costa et al. [7] and Maybury et al. [22] – are not publicly available and can thus not be evaluated or verified by others. This is detrimental to the use of these solutions in practice. Even the evaluation of proposed techniques by their authors is missing in many publications, as is illustrated by a selection of techniques shown in Table 1. Even if an evaluation exists, the numbers for false positive and detection rates are not directly comparable, since most authors used different, often newly constructed, simulated data on insider activities. Furthermore, in addition to not having been evaluated using realistic datasets, there is also a lack of evaluation of their use in production environment, e. g. through field tests, which in some cases, like the system of honeypots and honeytokens by Spitzner [31], is the only way to properly evaluate a proposed countermeasure.

Table 1. Percentage of false positive and detection rates of a selection of insider attack detection mechanisms

Existing work	False positive rate	Detection rate
Honeypots [31]	-	-
ELICIT [20]	1.5	84.0
Unix commands [28]	6.7	69.3
Unix commands [21]	1.3	61.5
MS Windows [10]	-	-
MS Windows [17]	22.0	67.7
Psychology [12]	-	-
Ontology [7]	-	-

3.4 Post-mortem Detection

The long-term objective consists in designing *preventive security mechanisms* against insider attacks. Unfortunately, it is questionable whether effective protection is achievable at all. However, *detecting attacks* (post-mortem) and identifying the culprit (attribution) might be sufficient to deter insiders in practice.

Thus, a potential avenue of research is to focus on detecting insider attacks. Existing technical approaches, as described in Sect. 2.2, focus on data collection, user profiling and anomaly detection. However, inside attackers typically have extensive access rights (especially if they are system administrators) and possess detailed knowledge about the IT infrastructure of their organisation, which endows them with the capability of changing data, manipulating user profiles and hiding their activities. A (debatable) approach is to deploy a comprehensive logging infrastructure that monitors the behaviour of all users and systems from a number of vantage points. This allows the examination of specific events from many different point of views of a system and makes it harder for attackers to cover their tracks, as they would have to manipulate logs in many different places in a consistent manner. Manipulating logs of one vantage point would in turn generate traces in other logs, leading to detectable inconsistencies that make it possible to verify the veracity [11] of the information presented in logs.

4   Challenges

In the following, we will show some challenges which will have to be solved in order to create an effective detection and prevention system for insider attacks.

4.1 Techniques for Post-mortem Detection of Insider Attacks

One of these challenges is the *automatic detection of insider attacks* based on log data and contextual information collected by the system. In addition to data collected from IT systems, data available from physical security systems could also be considered, such as biometrical access control systems or motion detectors, which could provide information about suspicious "offline" activities (e. g. access to server rooms at unusual times) and help with attributing activity to specific users. Algorithms from the field of anomaly detection will have to be adapted to this scenario. Special attention needs to be paid to the number of false positives generated by the anomaly detection algorithms, as even seemingly low false positive rates can lead to the number of false positives vastly exceeding the number of true positives [2], which may cause true positives to be shrugged off as "yet another false alarm".

4.2   Data Protection

The most important challenge for the implementation of a comprehensive logging system (as described in Sect. 3.4) is *sufficient data protection*. As the system would continuously monitor and log activities of all employees, the data produced by it would have to be protected in order to comply with data protection laws concerning employment. Insufficient protection may lead to the data being misused for surveillance of employees. Additionally, the system might also log sensitive data related to customers. Therefore, any information that could be used to identify persons (customers or employees) should be obfuscated (e. g. by pseudonyms as proposed and argued in the context of internal fraud screening by Flegel [8]) or removed altogether. It should only be possible to reverse this in case of a suspected security incident and it should not be possible for a single person to link log entries to persons.

A possible way of ensuring the consent of multiple parties before information is de-anonymised would be the use of a threshold decryption scheme. These schemes require a minimum number of private keys – but not necessarily all that are part of the scheme – to be present to decrypt data previously encrypted using a public key [29]. A similar approach has been developed by Armknecht and Dewald [1] in the context of digital forensics on sensitive e-mail data.

In some cases, partly de-anonymising data before applying anomaly detection algorithms to it may be necessary to be able to detect attacks at all. An example of this are login attempts on a server, where the IP address or at least information about the geographical location of the computer trying to connect would be relevant for detecting anomalies. On the other hand, even incomplete de-anonymisation may lead to linkability of certain types of behaviour to individual employees, invading their privacy. This shows that there is a trade-off between improved detectability of some attacks and user privacy related to how thoroughly the data used for anomaly detection is anonymised. Experiments will have to be performed to evaluate the impact of different forms and extents of anonymisation on the detectability of insider attacks. A similar trade-off exists in intrusion detection on network traces and has been discussed by Lakkaruja and Slagell [16] as well as Lundin and Jonsson [19]. Compared to detection of incoming attacks by intrusion detction systems, privacy is significantly more important in insider attack detection, as the data used for it will focus on the contextual information and activities of an organisation's employees, which are using the system over a long period of time, thus making it relatively easy to build profiles of them for illegitimate purposes.

Before systems for the detection and prevention of insider attacks can be used in practice, a sweet spot on this trade-off will have to be found. If no anonymisation was performed, these systems could not be used in practice at all in many legislations, as the privacy of employees and/or customers would be invaded. On the other hand, total anonymisation will likely remove too much information for the system to be of any help in tackling insider attacks. One way to solve this dilemma may be to adapt solutions that allow anonymity to be revoked under certain conditions [15].

4.3   Realistic Datasets for Evaluation of Detection Techniques

Another challenge is to create publicly available datasets which can be used to evaluate and improve detection and prevention techniques for insider attacks. As outlined in Sect. 3.2, there is currently a lack of such datasets. One possible way of obtaining a dataset would be to capture it in a real production environment that may be affected by insider attacks, i.e. a corporate or government network. However, it is unlikely that such organisations would be willing to let researchers capture a comprehensive dataset, as this would reveal all activity conducted within the organisation's IT infrastructure. This would make it necessary to remove or replace all confidential information from the dataset, which in itself poses a challenging research problem. Even if one was to find a way to achieve this, it is likely that the anonymisation would impact detection and prevention techniques, leading to the dataset potentially not resembling the real environment closely enough, rendering it useless for evaluation purposes.

With capturing data within an organisation's network being unrealistic, simulation remains as a way of generating a publicly available dataset. The challenge here is to make sure that a synthetically generated dataset resembles real world environments closely enough to allow evaluation of detection and prevention techniques as well as to provide means of robust comparability between different countermeasures.

5   Conclusion

In this paper, we analyse the current state of the art in insider attack detection and prevention and show some potential avenues of future research as well as challenges in the field. Our analysis has shown that existing security mechanisms cannot prevent insider attacks reliably. Detection and attribution is complicated by the ability of insiders to cover their tracks and fabricate evidence. Therefore, designing effective preventive, reactive and forensic techniques seems to be a fruitful area of future research.

Advances towards more effective techniques are hindered by a lack of unified definitions in the field and no datasets being publicly available that resemble real production environments closely enough to allow a comparative evaluation of techniques. Furthermore, previous research often ignores data protection and does not take the trade-off between detectability of insider attacks and protection of employee data into account.

References

1. Armknecht, F., Dewald, A.: Privacy-preserving email forensics. Digital Investigation 14(Suppl. 1), 127–136 (2015). http://www.sciencedirect.com/science/article/pii/S1742287615000481 (the Proceedings of the Fifteenth Annual DFRWS Conference)
2. Axelsson, S.: The base-rate fallacy and the difficulty of intrusion detection. ACM Trans. Inf. Syst. Secur. 3(3), 186–205 (2000)
3. Bundeskriminalamt: Polizeilich erfasste flle von cyberkriminalitt im engeren sinne in deutschland von 2000 bis 2014. Statista – Das Statisktik-Portal (2014). http://de.statista.com/statistik/daten/studie/295265/umfrage/polizeilich-erfasste-faelle-von-cyberkriminalitaet-im-engeren-sinne-in-deutschland/
4. Centre for the Protection of National Infrastructure: Ongoing personnel security: A good practise guide (2014). http://www.cpni.gov.uk/documents/publications/2014/2014006-ongoing-personal-security.pdf?epslanguage=en-gb
5. CERT Insider Threat Center: 2014 U.S. State of Cybercrime Survey (2014). http://resources.sei.cmu.edu/library/asset-view.cfm?assetID=298318
6. Coles-Kemp, L., Theoharidou, M.: Insider threat and information security management. In: Probst, C.W., Hunker, J., Gollmann, D., Bishop, M. (eds.) Insider Threats in Cyber Security, pp. 45–71. Springer, New York (2010)
7. Costa, D.L., Collins, M.L., Perl, S.J., Albrethsen, M.J., Silowash, G.J., Spooner, D.L.: An ontology for insider threat indicators. In: 10th International Conference on Semantic Technology for Intelligence, Defense, and Security (STIDS) (2015). http://resources.sei.cmu.edu/library/asset-view.cfm?assetid=426803
8. Flegel, U.: Privacy compliant internal fraud screening. In: Pohlmann, N., Reimer, H., Schneider, W. (eds.) ISSE 2010 Securing Electronic Business Processes, pp. 191–199. Vieweg+Teubner (2011)
9. Flynn, L., Huth, C., Trzeciak, R., Buttles-Valdez, P.: Best practices against insider threats in all nations. Technical report CMU/SEI-2013-TN-023, Software Engineering Institute, Carnegie Mellon University, Pittsburgh, PA (2013). http://resources.sei.cmu.edu/library/asset-view.cfm?AssetID=59082
10. Goldring, T.: User profiling for intrusion detection in windows NT. In: Proceedings of the 35th Symposium on the Interface (2003)
11. Gollmann, D.: Veracity, plausibility, and reputation. In: Askoxylakis, I., Pöhls, H.C., Posegga, J. (eds.) WISTP 2012. LNCS, vol. 7322, pp. 20–28. Springer, Heidelberg (2012)
12. Greitzer, F.L., Frincke, D.A.: Combining traditional cyber security audit data with psychosocial data: towards predictive modeling for insider threat mitigation. In: Probst, C.W., Hunker, J., Gollmann, D., Bishop, M. (eds.) Insider Threats in Cyber Security, pp. 85–113. Springer, New York (2010)
13. Hunker, J., Probst, C.W.: Insiders and insider threats - an overview of definitions and mitigation techniques. J. Wirel. Mob. Netw. Ubiquitous Comput. Dependable Appl. 2(1), 4–27 (2011)

14. Kaplan, J.M., Bailey, T., O'Halloran, D., Marcus, A., Chris, R.: Beyond Cybersecurity: Protecting Your Digital Business. Wiley, New York (2015)
15. Köpsell, S., Wendolsky, R., Federrath, H.: Revocable anonymity. In: Müller, G. (ed.) ETRICS 2006. LNCS, vol. 3995, pp. 206–220. Springer, Heidelberg (2006)
16. Lakkaraju, K., Slagell, A.J.: Evaluating the utility of anonymized network traces for intrusion detection. In: Levi, A., Liu, P., Molva, R. (eds.) 4th International ICST Conference on Security and Privacy in Communication Networks, SECURECOMM 2008, Istanbul, Turkey, September 22–25, 2008, p. 17. ACM (2008)
17. Li, L., Manikopoulos, C.N.: Windows nt one-class masquerade detection. In: Proceedings from the Fifth Annual IEEE SMC Information Assurance Workshop, pp. 82–87. IEEE Computer Society, June 2004
18. Lindemann, J.: Towards abuse detection and prevention in iaas cloud computing. In: Proceedings of the 10th International Conference on Availability, Reliability and Security (ARES 2015). IEEE Computer Society (2015)
19. Lundin, E., Jonsson, E.: Anomaly-based intrusion detection: privacy concerns and other problems. Comput. Netw. **34**(4), 623–640 (2000). http://dx.doi.org/10.1016/S1389-1286(00)00134--1
20. Maloof, M.A., Stephens, G.D.: ELICIT: a system for detecting insiders who violate need-to-know. In: Kruegel, C., Lippmann, R., Clark, A. (eds.) RAID 2007. LNCS, vol. 4637, pp. 146–166. Springer, Heidelberg (2007)
21. Maxion, R., Townsend, T.: Masquerade detection augmented with error analysis. Trans. Reliab. **53**(1), 124–147 (2004)
22. Maybury, M., Chase, P., Cheikes, B., Brackney, D., Matzner, S., Hetherington, T., Wood, B., Sibley, C., Marin, J., Longstaff, T.: Analysis and detection of malicious insiders. Technical report, DTIC Document (2005). http://oai.dtic.mil/oai/oai?verb=getRecord&metadataPrefix=html&identifier=ADA456356
23. Michelberg, K., Schive, L., Pollard, N.: Us cybercrime: Rising risks, reduced readiness – key findings from the 2014 us state of cybercrime survey (2014). https://www.pwc.com/us/en/increasing-it-effectiveness/publications/2014-us-state-of-cybercrime.html
24. Neumann, P.G.: Combatting insider threats. In: Probst, C.W., Hunker, J., Gollmann, D., Bishop, M. (eds.) Insider Threats in Cyber Security, pp. 17–44. Springer, New York (2010)
25. Pfleeger, C.P.: Reflections on the insider threat. In: Stolfo, S.J., Bellovin, S.M., Keromytis, A.D., Hershkop, S., Smith, S.W., Sinclair, S. (eds.) Insider Attack and Cyber Security, Advances in Information Security, vol. 39, pp. 5–16. Springer, New York (2008). http://dx.doi.org/10.1007/978-0-387-77322-3_5
26. Huysmans, P., Bellens, D., Van Nuffel, D., Ven, K.: Aligning the constructs of enterprise ontology and normalized systems. In: Albani, A., Dietz, J.L.G. (eds.) CIAO! 2010. LNBIP, vol. 49, pp. 1–15. Springer, Heidelberg (2010)
27. Salem, M.B., Hershkop, S., Stolfo, S.J.: A survey of insider attack detection research. In: Stolfo, S.J., Bellovin, S.M., Keromytis, A.D., Hershkop, S., Smith, S.W., Sinclair, S. (eds.) Insider Attack and Cyber Security. Advances in Information Security, vol. 39, pp. 69–90. Springer, US (2008). http://dx.doi.org/10.1007/978-0-387-77322-3_5
28. Schonlau, M., DuMouchel, W., Ju, W.H., Karr, A.F., Theus, M., Vardi, Y.: Computer intrusion: detecting masquerades. Stat. Sci. **16**(1), 58–74 (2001)
29. Shoup, V.: Practical threshold signatures. In: Preneel, B. (ed.) EUROCRYPT 2000. LNCS, vol. 1807, pp. 207–220. Springer, Heidelberg (2000)

30. Silowash, G., Cappelli, D., Moore, A., Trzeciak, R., Shimeall, T., Flynn, L.: Common sense guide to mitigating insider threats. Technical report, CMU/SEI-2012-TR-012, Software Engineering Institute, Carnegie Mellon University, Pittsburgh, PA (2012). http://resources.sei.cmu.edu/library/asset-view.cfm?AssetID=34017
31. Spitzner, L.: Honeypots: catching the insider threat. In: 19th Annual Computer Security Applications Conference, 2003, Proceedings, pp. 170–179. IEEE Computer Society, December 2003
32. Zimmermann, S.: Wirtschaftsspionage - Gefahr im eigenen Haus (2015). http://dw.de/p/1FPAo

Intrusion Detection in the Smart Grid Based on an Analogue Technique

Hartmut Richthammer and Sebastian Reif[✉]

Department Business Information Systems IV - IT Security Management,
University of Regensburg, Regensburg, Germany
{Hartmut.Richthammer,Sebastian.Reif}@ur.de

Abstract. In Smart Grid a customer's privacy is threatened by the fact that an attacker could deduce personal habits from the detailed consumption data. We analysed the publications in this field of research and found out that privacy does not seem to be the main focus. To verify this guess, we analysed it with the technique of directed graphs. This indicates that privacy isn't yet sufficiently investigated in the Smart Grid context. Hence we suggest a decentralised IDS based on NILM technology to protect customer's privacy. Thereby we would like to initiate a discussion about this idea.

Keywords: Smart grid · Smart meter · Intrusion detection system · IDS · NILM · Privacy

1 Introduction

During the last years power supply was subject to fundamental changes. In the course of the energy revolution the percentage of fossil fuels and nuclear power decreases and in return the percentage of renewable energies, such as wind and sun, increases. Therefore the energy production is more and more decentralized and the availability changes from static to dynamic. In this context not only a few actors of the infrastructure, e.g. the energy service provider, produce power but also private customers are able to act as producers by installing their own power supplies, e.g. photovoltaics, at their houses. It is also possible to store the power, e.g. in accumulators of electric cars. The former consumer acts as a producer and energy provider as well. We call him *Prosumer*.

To face these new challenges the SG infrastructure concept was established. Due to the increased number of producers it has to be ensured, that the network is not damaged by big deviations of power. In this context detailed consumption data of the *Prosumers* are recorded and sent by the smart meters to the energy service provider. This recorded data threatens the privacy of the *Prosumer*. The SG infrastructure is additionally threatened by external attackers [16,19].

S. Reif—The research leading to these results was supported by "Bavarian State Ministry of Education, Science and the Arts" as part of the FORSEC research association (http://www.bayforsec.de/).

© IFIP International Federation for Information Processing
Published by Springer International Publishing Switzerland 2016. All Rights Reserved
J. Camenisch and D. Kesdoğan (Eds.): iNetSec 2015, LNCS 9591, pp. 56–67, 2016.
DOI: 10.1007/978-3-319-39028-4_5

It is eligible, to detect these attacks by suitable IDS considering *Prosumer*'s privacy. In this paper a new approach is introduced.

2   Related Work

We investigated the number of available publications searched by Key Word and Key Word combinations. The queries were based on the IEEE Xplore® Digital Library. We think that this database is a quite important one for the research on SG. Nevertheless this restriction is a drawback of our work. In future analyses the search should be extended to other libraries such as Springer or Google Scholar.

2.1   Quantitative Analysis

The results gives us a first impression about the focus of actual research on SG and are illustrated in Tables 1 and 2.

The tables show that Smart Grid and privacy with over $10,000$ and $20,000$ hits respectively are important fields of research besides security.

To find interconnections between different Key Words, we searched for combinations of these terms, Table 2 shows hits on such combinations.

It could be concluded that the research on Smart Grid is mainly focused on security, but privacy is discussed less. Nonetheless protection of privacy in the context of SG is well analysed by many publications [8,10,15,18,23,25], IDS and attack vectors on SG are part of the current research [2,3,21,26,27] as well. The combination of the Key Words *Smart Grid, Intrusion Detection* and *Privacy* yields just five publications. It seems that especially privacy in connection with Intrusion Detection for the Smart Grid is not considered sufficiently. IDS aggregate and analyse a lot of data [6] and in addition this data is highly privacy relevant. The consumption data reveals details about the daily routine, consumer behaviour and habits of the residents [12,22,23]. However it seems that hitherto IDS is primarily used to protect the energy service provider not the Prosumer. Therefore we think that research with regard to the Prosumer's privacy should be intensified.

Table 1. Hits per Key Word (IEEE Xplore® digital library).

Key Word	Hits
Smart Grid	10,702
Privacy	20,952
Fraud	1435
Theft	1071
Intrusion detection	9,088
Advanced metering infrastructure	400
Security	126,852

Table 2. Hits per Key Word combinations (IEEE Xplore® digital library).

Key Word combination	Hits
Smart Grid, Security	1,502
Smart Grid, Privacy	288
Smart Grid, Advanced Metering Infrastructure, Security	84
Smart Grid, Intrusion Detection	52
Smart Grid, Advanced Metering Infrastructure, Privacy	30
Smart Grid, Advanced Metering Infrastructure, Privacy, Security	22
Smart Grid, Advanced Metering Infrastructure, Intrusion Detection	7
Smart Grid, Intrusion Detection, Privacy	5
Smart Grid, Intrusion Detection, Theft, Security	4
Smart Grid, Advanced Metering Infrastructure, Theft, Security	4
Smart Grid, Advanced Metering Infrastructure, Privacy, Theft	4
Smart Grid, Advanced Metering Infrastructure, Theft, Security, Intrusion Detection	4
Smart Grid, Advanced Metering Infrastructure, Theft, Privacy, Security	4

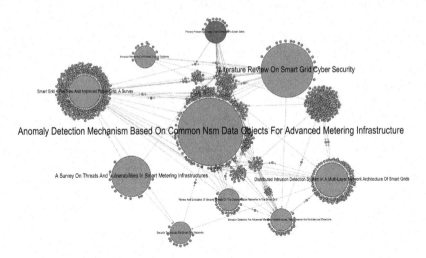

Fig. 1. Closeness Centrality of selected survey papers

2.2   Qualitative Analysis by Directed Graphs

To measure the impact of single publications we generated a network with directed graphs that shows the interconnections between different papers and their references. Thereby we tried to verify the assumptions we made above. For this purpose the results were processed to more meaningful graphs. We used the "Closeness Centrality" metric, which measures how far a node is away from other ones. A high value means that the publication and their references use lot of third party references. This suggests that they are survey papers and it is confirmed by a close look. These papers are represented by the nodes shown in Fig. 1. The node size visualises the closeness centrality value. The red coloured nodes represent publications that are related to privacy. As you can see, there is just one node of relevance, which is related to the topic privacy. This affirms our assumptions that privacy is not yet sufficiently investigated.

3   NILM Based IDS

NILM was first proposed by Hart [14] in the year 1989. The idea behind this concept is to use only one measurement device to gather consumption data of the whole household. It will be described in Sect. 3.3.

First we will introduce the infrastructure, the interconnection from a household with the SG itself and the IDS components in detail.

3.1   The Smart Meter Intrustion Detection Infrastructure

In Sect. 2 we have shown that privacy seems not to be an important part for IDS in the SG. The suggested concepts only analyse network traffic [29] and gather information outside the household [2]. Energy fraud and malicious devices which produce unusual consumption of energy are not detected. Salinas et al. [27] introduced an interesting concept for privacy-preserving energy theft detection, where the neighbourhood is involved in the fraud detection. But this concept does not consider the attacker inside a household.

Our approach is a privacy friendly inhouse IDS and was inspired by this idea. We want to reach this goal by developing a decentralized IDS where all relevant energy consumption data is aggregated by a device inside the household. This device should act as central AMS, illustrated in Fig. 2. Every available appliance inside a household is therefore known by the AMS, which is also the SM. Thus it can be avoided that sensitive data is permanently transferred to the energy service provider. The *Prosumers* produces and consumes energy which is depicted as a bidirectional energy flow in the figure. The energy flows through the SM and also bidirectional into the grid. Only the energy flow from the ESP is unidirectional. The data communication between every party is always bidirectional and should be encrypted in accord with the BSI [4].

All appliances consume energy and hence are directly connected with the SM over the powerline. Which leads to that the SM knows the energy consumption behaviour of the household. Inside the SM the following components should be included as it is recommended by the BSI:

– Some kind of user interaction component, where the consumer can monitor his energy consumpiton, ideally as historical graph.
– A TPM which implements a random generator and securely handles the private keys for decryption and signing.
– A communication module which handles the dataflow between the parties.

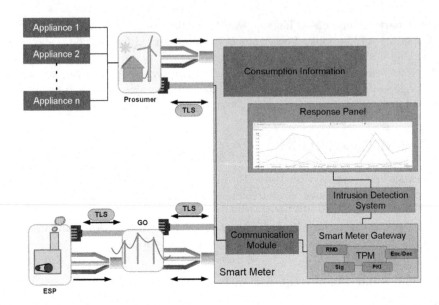

Fig. 2. Exemplary depiction of a Smart Meter Intrustion Detection Infrastructure. (Some parts of the graphic are from Marekich (Wikipedia) under the CC BY-SA 3.0 licence)

Our approach is to include the IDS and a response mechanism inside the SM. The user now has the possibility to get Informations about security incidents and react on them. How the data is collected and processed will be described in Sect. 3.3. The response system could be an LCD panel, a SMS or E-Mail sender, a web interface or an API where a third party device (e.g. Smartphone App) can connect to.

To detect, categorize and manage all energy consuming household appliances, an analogue technique like NILM could be used. Every device is identified by its individual energy consumption signature. The idea is, when every appliance can be identified inside a household and the normal energy consumption behaviour of a device or the whole system is known, an irregular acting device can be identified. For example a possible attack on an SG could be that high energy consuming devices (e.g. a air conditioning) in a specific region are compromised by a virus. What if all these devices are activated at the same time? A sharply rising energy consumption in this region would be the consequence. If we have a large region and the peak is high enough or the consumption goes over a long period of time, the grid structure could be overstressed and damaged. The data link communication between the malicious device and an attacker can be disguised in the normal internet traffic or over a encrypted communication. But an AMS with an integrated IDS could detect such an irregular energy consumption and counteract it, because an attacker can not hide the irregular energy consumption from the SM.

3.2 IDS Structure

Figure 3 shows examplary the information flow for the IDS structure. A system training phase is nessesary before the system can be deployed. A preparation module with a initial dataset trains the IDS. When this phase is finished, the protected system is monitored by an *IDS Module* which is inside the SM. For every incident the respone and notification module is triggered. The user can now interact with the system and give response in an appropriate manner. To deal with *false positives* or *false negatives* a feedback channel to the preparation module could be used to adjust the IDS. A detailed structure of the *IDS Module* itself is shown in Fig. 4. The *IDS Knowledge Database* contains the normal behaviour pattern of the household and the appliances. It provides the *Sensor* with information about the normal and abnormal behaviour. A second database

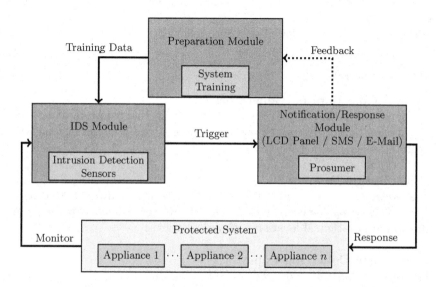

Fig. 3. Intrusion detection system information flow diagram [7].

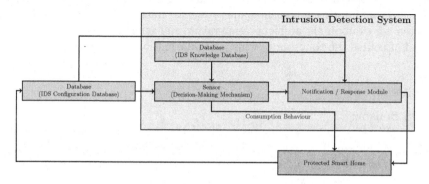

Fig. 4. Intrusion detection system module details [5]

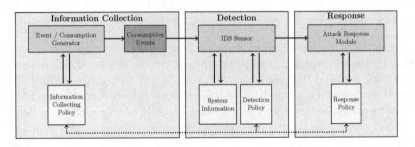

Fig. 5. Intrusion detection system policies [20].

(IDS Configuration Database) could contain IDS specific configuration information (e.g. in wich time frame the system should be active). The *Attack Response Module* was already described.

Figure 5 gives an overview about the policy structure from the IDS. The structure is seperated in three parts.

Information Collection

- **Event / Consumption Generator:**
  The generator is the physical device which collects the real world data. It uses the *Information Collecting Policy* to decide how the information and which information should be collected.

- **Consumption Events:**
  The *Consumption Events* are the resulting data which are generated by the *Event / Consumption Generator*. The events are handled by a storage process and stored in a central location such as a database.

- **Information Collecting Policy:**
  The *Information Collecting Policy* defines how information and which information will be collected. For example the collection intervall which characterizes the period between every collected energy consumption measurement. An external information such as meterological information could also be collected, for example the ambient temperature and general weather information. And of course the timestemp, when the information is collected.

Detection

- **IDS Sensor:**
  The *IDS Sensor* analyse the preserved information and tries to detect suspicious or abnormal behaviour. How the collected data is processed is defined by the *Detection Policy*. Also additional *System Information* can be considered for the data analysis by the sensor.

- **System Information:**
  To support the *IDS Sensor* during the detection process and the to decide if an anomaly is an attack or a false positive / false negative, additional information for example actual meterological information like the temperature could be used. The *System Information* privide such kind of information.

- **Detection Policy:**
  The *Detection Policy* specifies to which extent the energy flow will be monitored and stored. The *Detection Policy* could also define a value how detailed the collected data is analysed. The policy could also define which algorithm (for example which ML algorithm) is used to process the data. The policy also contains information how the determined results should be interpreted.

Response

- **Attack Response Module:**
  This module contacts the *Prosumer* and informs him or her about an incident. The user can now react on this event and can decide the next steps.

- **Response Policy:**
  The policy defines how, when and who gets informed about incidents. For example just the *Prosumer* gets informed or also a centralised database as descriped in Sect. 4. The information to the user could be commited over SMS, as an E-Mail, over a web interface or an API and a connected Smartphone Application.

The policies could be connected to attach conditions or to sum them up.

3.3   How NILM Works

As described before, every device should be identified and be known by the sytem. At least an abnormal behaviour should be detected. NILM is a concept which can fulfill these requirement. The idea of NILM is over 25 years old and there were many different NILM algorithms and concepts developed since.

We will give a short overview about NILM and how it works. The functionality can be classified in three main principles:

- In the *first* step, characteristic consumption or production data of appliances has to be collected. This means that the overall energy consumption of a household is measured and collected. The collection can be realised by external hardware or within a smart meter. The actual research distinguishes between two different collection methods, the high-frequency and low-frequency data collection. Though there is no exact definition of high-frequency and low-frequency [13, 24, 30, 31].

- In the *second* step, collected raw data has to be processed. This process is called *feature extraction*. Its goal is to generate an individual signature for every device [31]. A signature should be unique and describes a characteristic temporal change of consumption of each device. As a data base the real power and reactive power for a device can be used [1,9,28].
- After the raw data is analysed and signatures are generated, classification methods are used to disaggregate appliances in a *third* step. The classification can be separated in supervised and unsupervised classification. For the supervised method, labelled datasets are produced. This means that every generated signature is related to a device designation label which is set manually.

  In contrast, the unsupervised classification needs no external influence. This means that the device designation labels are already present in a pre-delivered database [11], are generated from the real power and reactive power plot or use a HMM and variations from this model, for example CFHMM [17].

4   Next Steps

Figure 6 depicts an example consumption trace. The red coloured graph shows the overall consumption of a household over a period of time. This trace is known by the SM. The other coloured traces symbolise the energy consumption of appliances inside a household and are inaccessible for the SM. The accumulated consumption of every device inside a household is represented by the overall consumption. If we are able to determine the consupmtion of every appliance, we are able to detect anomalies. Our next step will be the implementation of AMS, based on NILM technology. We want to find out which NILM concept works best for our IDS idea. Some NILM algorithms and concepts are based on ML algorithms. Our next research steps will go in this direction. We will

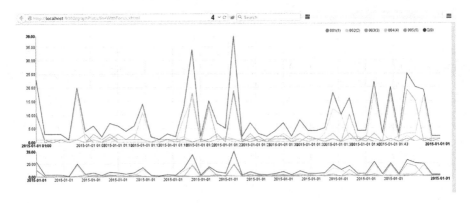

Fig. 6. Example of an energy consumption graph. The red line shows the overall consumption, the other colours show devices inside a household (Color figure online).

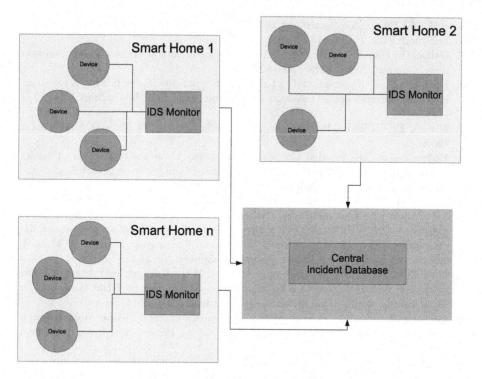

Fig. 7. Central incident database.

implement, train and test different ML concepts, based on energy consumption traces gathered in the real world.

For future ideas, the decentralised IDS could be combined with a centralised evaluation and analysis system, for example to detect false positives (Fig. 7). To come back to the air conditioning example, this could also be a false positive, caused by an unusual warm day. If the decentralised IDS of every household communicates incidents to a centralised system, false positives could be detected without revealing privacy relevant consumption data.

References

1. Baranski, M., Voss, J.: Genetic algorithm for pattern detection in NIALM systems. In: 2004 IEEE International Conference on Systems, Man and Cybernetics, vol. 4, pp. 3462–3468. IEEE (2004)
2. Berthier, R., Sanders, W.H., Khurana, H.: Intrusion detection for advanced metering infrastructures: requirements and architectural directions. In: 2010 First IEEE International Conference on Smart Grid Communications (SmartGridComm), pp. 350–355, October 2010
3. Berthier, R., Sanders, W.H.: Specification-based intrusion detection for advanced metering infrastructures. In: 2011 IEEE 17th Pacific Rim International Symposium on Dependable Computing (PRDC), pp. 184–193. IEEE (2011)

4. BSI. BSI Richtlinien SmartGrid BSI TR-03109-2 - Smart Meter Gateway Sicherheitsmodul Use Cases, March 2013
5. Debar, H., Dacier, M., Wespi, A.: Towards a taxonomy of intrusion-detection systems. Comput. Netw. **31**(8), 805–822 (1999)
6. Denning, D.E., Neumann, P.G.: Requirements and model for IDES - a real-time intrusion detection expert system. Document A005, SRI. International, vol. 333 (1985)
7. Dorosz, P., Kazienko, P.: Systemy wykrywania intruzw. VI Krajowa Konferencja (2002)
8. Efthymiou, C., Kalogridis, G.: Smart grid privacy via anonymization of smart metering data. In: 2010 First IEEE International Conference on Smart Grid Communications (SmartGridComm), pp. 238–243. IEEE (2010)
9. Figueiredo, M., De Almeida, A., Ribeiro, B.: Home electrical signal disaggregation for non-intrusive load monitoring (NILM) systems. Neurocomput. **96**, 66–73 (2012)
10. Garcia, F.D., Jacobs, B.: Privacy-friendly energy-metering via homomorphic encryption. In: Cuellar, J., Lopez, J., Barthe, G., Pretschner, A. (eds.) STM 2010. LNCS, vol. 6710, pp. 226–238. Springer, Heidelberg (2011)
11. Goncalves, H., Ocneanu, A., Berges, M., Fan, R.H.: Unsupervised disaggregation of appliances using aggregated consumption data. In: The 1st KDD Workshop on Data Mining Applications in Sustainability (SustKDD) (2011)
12. Greveler, U., Justus, B., Loehr, D.: Multimedia content identification through smart meter power usage profiles. In: Computers, Privacy and Data Protection (2012)
13. Gupta, S., Reynolds, M.S., Patel, S.N.: ElectriSense: single-point sensing using EMI for electrical event detection and classification in the home. In: Proceedings of the 12th ACM International Conference on Ubiquitous Computing, pp. 139–148. ACM (2010)
14. Hart, G.W.: Residential energy monitoring and computerized surveillance via utility power flows. Technol. Soc. Mag. IEEE **8**(2), 12–16 (1989)
15. Kalogridis, G., Efthymiou, C., Denic, S.Z., Lewis, T., Cepeda, R.: Privacy for smart meters : Towards undetectable appliance load signatures. In: 2010 First IEEE International Conference on Smart Grid Communications (SmartGridComm), pp. 232–237. IEEE (2010)
16. Khurana, H., Hadley, M., Ning, L., Frincke, D.A.: Smart-grid security issues. Secur. Priv. IEEE **8**(1), 81–85 (2010)
17. Kim, H., Marwah, M., Arlitt, M.F., Lyon, G., Han, J.: Unsupervised disaggregation of low frequency power measurements. In: SDM, vol. 11, pp. 747–758. SIAM (2011)
18. LeMay, M., Gross, G., Gunter, C.A., Garg, S.: Unified architecture for large-scale attested metering. In: 40th Annual Hawaii International Conference on System Sciences, HICSS 2007, pp. 115–124. IEEE (2007)
19. Lu, Z., Lu, X., Wang, W., Wang, C.: Review and evaluation of security threats on the communication networks in the smart grid. In: Military Communications Conference, MILCOM 2010, pp. 1830–1835, October 2010
20. Lundin, E., Jonsson, E.: Survey of intrusion detection research. Technical report, Chalmers University of Technology (2002)
21. McLaughlin, S., Holbert, B., Fawaz, A.-Q., Berthier, R., Zonouz, S.: A multi-sensor energy theft detection framework for advanced metering infrastructures. IEEE J. Sel. Areas Commun. **31**(7), 1319–1330 (2013)
22. Müller, K.: Gewinnung von Verhaltensprofilen am intelligenten Stromzähler. Datenschutz und Datensicherheit-DuD **34**(6), 359–364 (2010)

23. Molina-Markham, A., Shenoy, P., Fu, K., Cecchet, E., Irwin, D.: Private memoirs of a smart meter. In: Proceedings of the 2nd ACM Workshop on Embedded Sensing Systems for Energy-Efficiency in Building, pp. 61–66. ACM (2010)

24. Parson, O., Ghosh, S., Weal, M., Rogers, A.: An unsupervised training method for non-intrusive appliance load monitoring. Artif. Intell. **217**, 1–19 (2014)

25. Petrlic, R.: A privacy-preserving concept for smart grids. Sicherheit vernetzten Systemen **18**, B1–B14 (2010)

26. Salem, M.: Adaptive Real-time Anomaly-based Intrusion Detection using Data Mining and Machine Learning Techniques. Ph.D. thesis, Kassel, Univ., Diss. (2014)

27. Salinas, S., Li, M., Li, P.: Privacy-preserving energy theft detection in smart grids. In: 2012 9th Annual IEEE Communications Society Conference on Sensor, Mesh and Ad Hoc Communications and Networks (SECON), pp. 605–613, June 2012

28. Streubel, R., Yang, B.: Identification of electrical appliances via analysis of power consumption. In: 2012 47th International on Universities Power Engineering Conference (UPEC), pp. 1–6. IEEE (2012)

29. Valdes, A., Cheung, S.: Intrusion monitoring in process control systems. In: 42nd Hawaii International Conference on System Sciences, HICSS 2009, pp. 1–7. IEEE (2009)

30. Zeifman, M., Roth, K.: Nonintrusive appliance load monitoring: Review and outlook. IEEE Trans. Consum. Electron. **57**(1), 76–84 (2011)

31. Zoha, A., Gluhak, A., Imran, M., Rajasegarar, S.: Non-intrusive load monitoring approaches for disaggregated energy sensing: a survey. Sensors **12**(12), 16838–16866 (2012)

Anonymous Communication

On Building Onion Routing into Future Internet Architectures

Daniele E. Asoni[✉], Chen Chen, David Barrera, and Adrian Perrig

Network Security Group, Department of Computer Science,
ETH Zürich, Zurich, Switzerland
daniele.asoni@inf.ethz.ch

Abstract. User privacy on the Internet has become a pressing concern in recent years largely due to the revelations of large scale network surveillance programs. Research initiatives around future Internet architectures (FIAs) offer a unique opportunity to integrate privacy protection measures into the architecture of the network itself. In this paper, we survey the main design challenges of network layer onion routing protocols in FIAs. We empirically investigate the requirements and trade-offs of different design choices. Our goal is to identify promising research directions and incentivize further exploration of the field.

1   Introduction

Recent revelations about global-scale pervasive surveillance [13] programs have demonstrated that Internet users' privacy is severely threatened. These revelations suggest massive amounts of private traffic, including web browsing activities, location information, and personal communications are being harvested in bulk by domestic and foreign intelligence agencies. In response to these threats, an increasing number of privacy-concerned users are resorting to anonymity tools and services. The state-of-the-art solutions today are onion routing systems (most notably Tor [11]), which try to strike a balance between privacy and performance, enabling low-latency anonymous communication suitable for typical Internet activities (e.g., web browsing and instant messaging). Many of these systems work on top of the Internet as overlay networks: they rely on a number of servers, typically provided and run by volunteers, which anonymize user traffic by relaying it across the network a number of times. While these systems are gaining popularity, the active number of users still represents only a small fraction of the entire Internet population, partly because of these systems' limitations in terms of latency and scalability.

In recent years, to overcome the performance and scalability limitations of traditional anonymity systems, researchers have explored a new approach: building anonymity systems directly *into* the network architecture [6,10,20,23,28]. Instead of relying on volunteer-run servers, these proposals require Internet routers to perform traffic anonymization in addition to their typical

© IFIP International Federation for Information Processing
Published by Springer International Publishing Switzerland 2016. All Rights Reserved
J. Camenisch and D. Kesdoğan (Eds.): iNetSec 2015, LNCS 9591, pp. 71–81, 2016.
DOI: 10.1007/978-3-319-39028-4_6

packet forwarding operations. Current research in Future Internet Architectures (FIAs) [17,33,34] gives the opportunity to concretely plan for and evaluate this paradigm shift.

Research on network-layer anonymity systems is still in its infancy. Only a small fraction of the design space has been explored so far, and many of the important challenges and design decisions in the field have not been analyzed in detail. This paper aims to help fill this gap by identifying the main problems that arise when designing such systems, and by analyzing the trade-offs brought by those design choices.

The remainder is organized as follows. Section 2 gives background about traditional anonymity systems, FIAs, and recent network-layer anonymity systems based on FIAs. In Sect. 3, we discuss the necessary considerations when defining a threat model for onion routing systems at the network layer, showing how performance requirements and the network topology itself bound the privacy guarantees that such systems can provide. In Sect. 4 we present a set of design challenges and propose possible solutions as well as potential research directions. We conclude in Sect. 5.

2   Background and Related Work

Network-layer anonymity systems are usually an adaptation of traditional overlay anonymity systems. Thus, many of the fundamental concepts remain the same in both types of systems. For this reason we begin by presenting the traditional systems, in particular focusing on mix networks and onion routing. We then describe relevant FIA-based proposals, and finally present recent research on network-layer anonymity systems.

2.1   Traditional Anonymity Systems

The first system designed to enable anonymous communication over the Internet was proposed by Chaum in 1981 [4]. The main idea in this system is as follows: an end-host (the *source*) wishing to communicate anonymously with another end-host (the *destination*) chooses a sequence of servers (generically called *nodes*) that will relay the traffic. We call this sequence a *path*. Additionally, the source encrypts each message it sends multiple times in such a way that every node on the path will be able to remove one layer of encryption, until the final node (or the destination) obtains the original message. This technique is called onion encryption. Since messages look different (as a result of encryption or decryption) before and after being processed by a node, and under the assumption that many users will send messages through the system, it is non-trivial for the adversary to trace messages and thus to de-anonymize the communicating parties.

Chaum's design also includes batching and mixing of messages at every node, which increase the difficulty for an adversary to trace those messages across the network. For this reason Chaum's system, and others that are based on the same principles [8,9,18], are called mix networks or mix-nets. These systems typically do on-the-fly key establishment for every message using the long-term public keys of the nodes on the path. Key negotiations, together with batching and mixing, make mix-nets very slow, and thus suitable only for latency-tolerant applications like email.

The other important category of anonymity systems, which derives from mix-nets, is that of onion routing systems. The main examples are Tor [11], I2P [32] and JonDonym [14,22]. These systems also use onion encryption, but they typically do not perform mixing or batching to avoid the performance penalty. They also create *circuits* (also called tunnels or sessions), i.e., they establish shared keys with each node on the path, and then use these keys to send many messages/packets over the same path. The overall speed of onion routing systems means that, unlike mix-nets, they can be used for applications like web browsing and instant messaging. The drawback of these systems is that they provide weaker security guarantees, which are typically expressed by considering threat models with more limited adversaries.

Likely due to their low latency, (circuit-based) onion routing systems are the most used anonymous networks today. Furthermore, the network-layer anonymity systems described in Sect. 2.3 are also mostly based on onion routing.

2.2   Future Internet Architectures

In response to the problems that the current Internet is facing, a number of research initiatives were started with the goal of defining new network architectures for the next-generation Internet [26]. As research in re-defining the Internet is still ongoing, there is an opportunity to integrate support for privacy-enhancing technologies into the network architecture itself.

Some of the new architectures that have been proposed already include features which can be leveraged by anonymity networks (though the reason for their inclusion in the design lies strictly in networking aspects). In particular, some of these FIAs grant the end hosts a certain degree of control over the path that their traffic takes to traverse the network [17,31,34]. Control, or at least knowlege of the path, is typically offered at the granularity of Autonomous Systems (ASes) or Internet Service Providers (ISPs). Control and visibility of network paths is a fundamental property leveraged by network-layer onion routing systems, with the main realization being that intermediate ISPs and/or ASes can act as nodes to perform traffic anonymization. Assuming that the ISPs and ASes have public cryptographic keys that can be obtained and verified by the source, it is even possible for the source to negotiate keys with the nodes on the path to perform cryptographic operations on packets, (e.g., onion encryption [6]).

2.3   Network-Layer Anonymity Systems

The most practical and most used anonymity systems today are onion routing systems. However, application-layer overlay networks, on which today's onion routing systems are based, have inherent performance limitations. First, since each hop can traverse the entire network, the total propagation delay can be high.

Second, the end hosts' network stacks add substantial processing and queuing delay [12]. Finally, compared to ISP infrastructure, volunteer-run nodes typically offer only low to medium throughput [30].

Recent works have proposed to address the performance limitation of onion routing systems by building anonymity systems into the network layer [6,10, 20,23,28]. LAP [20] and Dovetail [28] (so-called *lightweight systems*) hide end hosts' network locations by concealing routing information. However, in these two protocols, packets remain unchanged as they traverse the network, making both schemes vulnerable to trivial packet matching attacks. In contrast, Tor instead of IP [23] and HORNET [6] advocate performing onion routing at the network layer, where Internet Service Providers (ISPs) assume the role of onion relays and support per-hop high-speed onion encryption/decryption.

We note that an important difference (and limitation) of network-layer anonymity system compared to overlay systems is that in the former the nodes typically only forward traffic to adjacent nodes. In overlay anonymity networks, on the other hand, it is assumed that each node can communicate with any other node. In Sect. 3 we show the limitations that this difference entails.

As discussed in Sect. 2.2, we assume that the network architecture provides end hosts with information about the network and the paths, which is a fundamental requirement of many of these network-layer anonymity systems. However, it is worth noting that LAP [20] differs from the other proposed schemes in this respect, as it does not require path information to be known to the source. The reason LAP does not rely on this assumption is that its privacy guarantees are weak: the source has no control over whether its traffic is truly anonymized, and has to fully trust its ISP. We discuss anonymity guarantees in the next section.

3   Threat Model Considerations

Traditionally, high-latency mix systems [4] consider powerful Dolev-Yao adversaries (i.e., adversaries that control the entire network), and typically try to guarantee the highest degree of anonymity. Defining a threat model that is as clear for low-latency onion routing systems is generally more difficult. Low-latency schemes are unable to defend against Dolev-Yao adversaries, and almost any observation of the network increases the knowledge of the adversary, thereby affecting anonymity. This means that the definition of anonymity needs to be quantitative [2], and this is a challenging task as it requires an analysis of the actual network topology and the entities involved. For this reason even the most popular anonymity systems provide only some approximate notion of what an adversary is allowed to do, and what guarantees the system provides for its users [11]. For network-layer anonymity systems these challenges remain, but additional elements must be considered.

Performance constraints. First, it is important to note that performance is a primary goal for network-layer low-latency anonymity systems. This implies, for example, that performing cryptographic operations on the packet should not constitute a bottleneck that limits a node's throughput. Some of the proposed

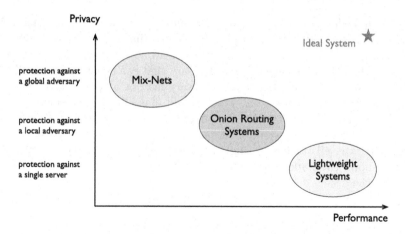

Fig. 1. Conceptual representation of the performance-privacy trade-off for anonymity systems, according to the categories described in Sect. 2 (figure adapted from Hsiao et al. [20]).

lightweight schemes [20, 28] lower the anonymity guarantees significantly in order to achieve better performance and scalability (see Fig. 1), by considering a weak threat model in which at most one node can be compromised. HORNET [6], an onion routing systems, tries to raise the bar, preserving user anonymity against more powerful adversaries, but has to sacrifice some performance. Unlike LAP and Dovetail, HORNET requires an initial circuit setup which involves expensive asymmetric cryptography operations, and data packets need to be fully onion encrypted/decrypted at each node. While the loss in performance is a clear downside of such a scheme, it appears to be unavoidable if the goal it to protect against stronger (and arguably more realistic) adversaries.

Topology constraints. Another important aspect of network-layer protocols is that they are constrained by the network topology and the business relations between network entities. This reduces the anonymity guarantees that such systems can provide [6], as sources are not free to choose arbitrary paths traversing the network (a property explicitly enabled by overlay systems). For example, in the extreme case where the source and destination are in the same ISP, complete de-anonymization is trivial if the ISP is malicious. This shows one of the important challenges in the definition of the threat model: typically low-latency anonymity systems require that an adversary should not be able to observe both source and destination. However, for a variety of reasons a user many not trust its own ISP, so in such cases the system does not provide any guarantees.[1]

Trust assumptions. Traditional onion routing protocols typically use secure channels between nodes to protect against eavesdroppers. Tor, for instance, specifies TLS connections to transmit data between pairs of relays. At the network

---

[1] It is possible to mitigate these restrictions by adding redirection in the network (see Sect. 4.5).

layer, an equivalent security mechanism would be some form of link encryption (e.g., IPsec [29]). In HORNET, the authors argue that link encryption may not be required under all network settings and for all adversaries. The reasoning is that if the threat model considers an adversary that can legally get access to the communication links, then the same adversary may be able to coerce ISPs into handing over all encryption keys, which would make link encryption pointless. However, should the threat model be different, it could be beneficial to use link encryption. One such case would be if multiple links between nodes, usually considered separate, all traverse a single Internet exchange Point (IXP) [21]. This example shows the importance of the threat model definition, which directly influences the design decisions.

4   Trade-Offs and Challenges in the Design Space

We now analyze some of the main design questions and challenges that arise when building onion routing systems at the network layer. While most of the items below concern performance, some of these design decisions also depend on the chosen threat model (see Sect. 3) and expected security guarantees.

4.1   Stateful vs. Stateless Node Design

To process and forward a packet, onion routing relays require state including cryptographic keys and routing information. In Tor, each relay node maintains the state for all the circuits traversing the relay. Given the high throughput and the limited amount of high-speed memory on routers, a stateful relay-node design creates scalability problems. We estimate, based on packet traces of an edge router [3], that a router with 100 Gb/s would need around 20 GB of state if all flows traversing through that router were Tor flows.

The ever decreasing costs of memory hardware might overcome the problem in the long term, but we note that to achieve high performance, routers need specialized high-speed memory, whose cost is higher than system memory. Furthermore, stored state is always a challenge for parallelization: if multiple cores need to access the same state, there are synchronization problems, and caching becomes less effective; if multiple machines need to access the same state, the state needs to be replicated. Hence, to mitigate such scalability problems in a stateful design, ISPs must either equip routers with a large high-speed memory, or carefully conduct load-balancing to delegate the state across multiple routers.

The diametrically opposed design choice is a stateless relay design, where each packet carries the necessary state embedded in its header [6,20,28]. However, the stateless design requires large packet headers, reducing the effective throughput; it also requires cryptographic schemes that protect packet-carried state from tampering, and prevent it from leaking information about end hosts. This leads to more complex designs which require additional cryptographic operations and whose security is more difficult to analyze (cf. the simplicity of Tor [11], which is stateful, with more complex design of HORNET [6], which is stateless).

4.2 Transport Control

Tor guarantees lossless and in-order delivery of packets by using reliable transport between neighboring relays. Although this scheme (based on TLS) enables the detection of malicious packet modification, replay, or dropping, it introduces a high overhead due to additional processing and queuing[2] [16]. In comparison, protocols without reliable per-hop transport control [6,20,28] can reach lower latency and high throughput, but they consider different (usually weaker) threat models.

Another disadvantage of having only end-to-end transport control is that the transport layer of the network stack is exposed to the remote endpoint. This can, for instance, allow a malicious destination to perform network stack fingerprinting (e.g., learn what operating system is running). Note, however, that regardless of the design, some part of the network stack is always exposed. For example, in Tor it is still possible to obtain information about the host at the application layer (e.g., HTTP).

4.3 Circuit Setup

Low-latency onion routing systems need to set up circuits, a process which typically involves asymmetric cryptographic operations. The established circuits are then used to forward traffic efficiently (i.e., using only symmetric key cryptography). Existing onion routing systems adopt one of two strategies for the circuit setup: telescopic setup and direct setup. The telescopic setup [11] consists in the extension of the circuit one hop at a time, so that the key exchange with the i-th node is completed before the $(i + 1)$-th node is contacted. The telescopic setup guarantees forward secrecy, but imposes high communication latency ($O(N^2)$), where N is the number of nodes on the path). Furthermore, this type of setup requires that the underlying FIA allow traffic to flow in both direction on all links, which might not always be the case [19].

The direct setup [6] does not suffer from these drawbacks. In particular, the communication latency is linear in N, but it cannot provide forward secrecy. Whether this is acceptable or not depends on the threat model: if it is assumed that the adversary will not be able to compromise certain nodes in the future, then a direct setup can be used. Otherwise it is still possible to mitigate the impact of a future compromise by changing circuit setup keys regularly. It can be challenging, however, to distribute the new keys if they are changed frequently. We note that direct setup does not preclude the end hosts from establishing an end to end channel that guarantees forward secrecy for the contents of the communication.

4.4 Bootstrapping Anonymous Communication

A difficult and still open problem is how to bootstrap anonymous communications in future Internet architectures. A source needs certain information to set

---

[2] Alternative transport designs have been studied to improve the performance of Tor in this respect [1,27], but the fundamental problem of queuing remains.

up circuits, which usually at least includes the address of the intended destination, of a path to that destination[3], and of the public keys of the nodes on that path. The challenge lies in retrieving this information in an anonymity-preserving way, while still providing the scalability and low latency properties of the main anonymity protocol (see Sect. 3).

Overlay anonymity systems (for instance, Tor) have an advantage in this case, because any sequence of mixes/onion relays can be used to reach any destination. This allows a source to construct a circuit without risking potential de-anonymization, as the circuit should give the attacker no information about the intended destination. Once the circuit is established, the source can ask the last mix/onion relay to perform the destination lookup through the established circuit. For onion routing protocols at the network layer this scheme cannot be directly applied, as the circuits are constructed on network paths which leak information about the source's location and the intended destination. We point out that this problem affects also the lightweight anonymity systems LAP [20] and Dovetail [28].

The simplest solution would be to use an overlay system only for bootstrapping, and then switch to a network layer onion routing system for the actual anonymous communication. The drawback of such a scheme would be a higher delay before the circuit is established, which is a problem for usability. Furthermore, the most popular anonymity systems today support a few million users a day [30], but if network anonymity protocols are used by a more significant fraction of the Internet population there might be scalability issues [6], so this option's feasibility requires further investigation.

Another possibility is to implement a broadcast mechanism which pushes all topology information (or a large part of it) to all users. Pathlet routing [17] might be used to achieve such a broadcasting system, as proposed by Sankey and Wright for Dovetail [28]. It is unclear whether such a system would scale to the size of the Internet, especially considering that public keys and certificates would also need to be broadcast. A more plausible scheme could be based on the idea of Federrath et al. [15], which combines a broadcasting mechanism for popular destinations with an overlay system for the rest.

For completeness we mention that there are systems that allow private information retrieval (PIR) [7], which means that a client is able to obtain information from a database without the database server knowing what piece of information is being accessed. Such systems could be used to solve certain parts of the problem, for example retrieval of the destinations address. However, such schemes impose high computational burden on servers, and while there have been some applications to anonymous communications [25], these do not appear to be well suited for our purposes.

---

[3] A path is made of a sequence of nodes that can route traffic from the source to the destination.

4.5   Hybrids Between Network-Layer and Overlay Anonymity Systems

To mitigate the problem of topology constraints (Sect. 3), Sankey and Wright [28] suggest that ISPs could deviate from the standard valley-freeness constraint[4] to allow some redirection. It is unclear, however, whether such a scenario would be deployable in practice, since it requires ISPs to use resources to forward traffic that is neither originating from, nor destined to, one of their clients. A similar, but more radical approach is to assume that a number of end hosts could act as proxies, and thus add an additional global redirection that would eliminate the problem. This approach is an example of combining network layer anonymity protocols with overlay systems, albeit with the drawback of increased in communication latency.

It may be desirable to allow the user (or software acting on the user's behalf) to select from a range of protocols for a specific connection. Such flexibility would allow clients to dynamically trade off performance and privacy as needed for each particular case and adversary. More research is needed to accurately classify protocols and connection types based on their performance and privacy guarantees.

4.6   Legal Issues and Deployment Incentives

To date, the research community has focused on the technical aspects of anonymity systems while largely neglecting the legal aspects and economical incentives for the entities who should deploy those systems. We argue that it is important to consider, at least at a high level, what legal obstacles network entities might face when trying to deploy anonymity systems, and what incentives these entities have for making such systems available to their customers. Indeed, even the most secure and high-performing system is pointless if it cannot be used, so it is worth considering these issues during technical protocol design.

ISPs may benefit from offering anonymity as a service to both their immediate subscribers and to subscribers of other ISPs, but ISPs must simultaneously comply with legal requirements (e.g., state-mandated data retention laws) to facilitate the investigation of criminal activity. A naive solution here is to build anonymity systems with so called "master keys" that ISPs or entities with judicial power can use to de-anonymize communicating parties. This approach, however, is prone to abuse which could lead to pervasive de-anonymization of all users.

A perhaps better-suited solution may be for ISPs to keep logs of users generating anonymous traffic, while not allowing the immediate de-anonymization of traffic. If legally compelled to de-anonymize traffic, the ISP can assist in

---

[4] Valley freeness is a routing property that derives from the fact that ISPs and ASes have an incentive to only forward traffic that either comes from, or is destined to, one of their customers. When this property holds, for example, no ISP reflects traffic arriving from outside the ISP back to where it originated.

recording anonymous traffic, possibly cooperating with neighboring ISPs. De-anonymization attempts can then be performed for specific points on the path.

The recently proposed cMix [5] system consists of a fixed sequence of mix nodes, and the authors suggest that each node could be run by a different nation: such a distributed system would guarantee that several legal domains must be involved and must agree on sharing information to de-anonymize single communications.

But while the technical community can find various options with different trade-offs, lawmakers should decide the correct balance between the right to privacy and free speech, as well clearly define the role played by law enforcement in cases where anonymous networks are used. Recent work [24] points out the need for further research on the legal questions that arise around anonymous communications. The sooner there is clarity on these matters, the sooner ISPs and other parties can decide whether to and how to invest into these technologies.

5   Conclusion

This paper has given an overview of the design considerations, trade-offs, and challenges in deploying onion routing anonymity systems on future Internet architectures. Recent research has shown that network-level anonymous networks are not only feasible in practice, but can provide better performance and better privacy to any application. As deployment of future Internet architectures gains momentum, we expect that these theoretical anonymous network proposals will begin to see real-world adoption. While more research is needed to further investigate these and other aspects, we hope the discussion herein will guide exploration of the design space, ultimately leading to more efficient and more secure anonymous networks.

References

1. AlSabah, M., Goldberg, I.: PCTCP: per-circuit TCP-over-IPsec transport for anonymous communication overlay networks. In: ACM CCS (2013)
2. Backes, M., Kate, A.: AnoA: a framework for analyzing anonymous communication protocols. In: IEEE CSF (2013)
3. CAIDA UCSD Anonymized Internet Traces 2014. Accessed 30 Apr 2015. http://www.caida.org/data/passive/passive_2014_dataset.xml
4. Chaum, D.L.: Untraceable electronic mail, return addresses, and digital pseudonyms. Commun. ACM **24**(2), 84–90 (1981)
5. Chaum, D., et al.: cMix: Anonymization by high-performance scalable mixing. Technical report (2016). https://eprint.iacr.org/2016/008
6. Chen, C., et al.: HORNET: High-speed Onion Routing at the Network Layer. In: ACM CCS (2015)
7. Chor, B., et al.: Private information retrieval. J. ACM **45**(6), 965–981 (1998)
8. Danezis, G., Dingledine, R., Mathewson, N.: Mixminion: Design of a Type III Anonymous Remailer Protocol. In: IEEE S&P (2003)

9. Danezis, G., Goldberg, I.: Sphinx: a compact and provably secure mix format. In: IEEE S&P (2009)
10. DiBenedetto, S., et al.: ANDaNA: anonymous named data networking application. In: NDSS (2011)
11. Dingledine, R., Mathewson, N., Syverson, P.: Tor: the second-generation onion router. In: USENIX Security (2004)
12. Dingledine, R., Murdoch, S.J.: Performance Improvements on Tor or, Why Tor is slow and what we're going to do about it. Technical report, The Tor Project (2009). https://research.torproject.org/techreports/performance-2009-11-09.pdf
13. Farrell, S., Tschofenig, H.: Pervasive Monitoring Is an Attack. IETF RFC 7258
14. Federrath, H.: AN.ON - Privacy protection on the Internet. ERCIM News **49**, 11 (2002)
15. Federrath, H., Fuchs, K.-P., Herrmann, D., Piosecny, C.: Privacy-preserving DNS: analysis of broadcast, range queries and mix-based protection methods. In: Atluri, V., Diaz, C. (eds.) ESORICS 2011. LNCS, vol. 6879, pp. 665–683. Springer, Heidelberg (2011)
16. Geddes, J., Jansen, R., Hopper, N.: IMUX: managing tor connections from two to infinity, and beyond. In: WPES (2014)
17. Godfrey, P.B., et al.: Pathlet routing. In: ACM SIGCOMM (2009)
18. Gülcü, C., Tsudik, G.: Mixing email with babel. In: NDSS (1996)
19. He, Y., et al.: On routing asymmetry in the internet. In: IEEE GLOBECOM (2005)
20. Hsiao, H.C., et al.: LAP: lightweight anonymity and privacy. In: IEEE S&P (2012)
21. Johnson, A., et al.: Users get routed: traffic correlation on tor by realistic adversaries. In: ACM CCS (2013)
22. JonDonym. Accessed 24 Feb 2016. https://anonymous-proxy-servers.net/
23. Liu, V., et al.: Tor instead of IP. In: ACM HotNets (2011)
24. Minarik, T., Osula, A.M.: Tor does not stink: Use and abuse of the Tor anonymity network from the perspective of law. Comput. Law Secur. Rev. **32**(1), 111–127 (2016)
25. Mittal, P., et al.: Scalable anonymous communication with provable security. In: USENIX HotSec (2010)
26. Pan, J., Paul, S., Jain, R.: A survey of the research on future internet architectures. IEEE Commun. Mag. **49**(7), 26–36 (2011)
27. Reardon, J., Goldberg, I.: Improving tor using a TCP-over-DTLS tunnel. In: USENIX Security (2009)
28. Sankey, J., Wright, M.: Dovetail: stronger anonymity in next-generation internet routing. In: De Cristofaro, E., Murdoch, S.J. (eds.) PETS 2014. LNCS, vol. 8555, pp. 283–303. Springer, Heidelberg (2014)
29. Seo, K., Kent, S.: Security architecture for the Internet protocol. IETF RFC 4301 (2005)
30. Tor Metrics. Accessed 13 May 2015. https://metrics.torproject.org
31. Yang, X., Clark, D., Berger, A.W.: NIRA: a new inter-domain routing architecture. IEEE/ACM Trans. Networking **15**(4), 775–788 (2007)
32. Zantout, B., Haraty, R.: I2P data communication system. In: ICN (2011)
33. Zhang, L., et al.: Named data networking. ACM SIGCOMM **44**(3), 66–73 (2014)
34. Zhang, X., et al.: SCION: scalability, control, and isolation on next-generation networks. In: IEEE S&P (2011)

Anonymity Online for Everyone: What Is Missing for Zero-Effort Privacy on the Internet?

Dominik Herrmann[1]([⊠]), Jens Lindemann[2], Ephraim Zimmer[2],
and Hannes Federrath[2]

[1] Institute for Information Systems, University of Siegen, Siegen, Germany
herrmann@wiwi.uni-siegen.de
[2] Computer Science Department, University of Hamburg, Hamburg, Germany
{jens.lindemann,ephraim.zimmer,
hannes.federrath}@informatik.uni-hamburg.de

Abstract. Privacy is difficult to protect on the Internet, because surveillance is ubiquitous. Researchers have conceived many different countermeasures. However, these solutions have so far failed to find widespread adoption due to poor performance and usability. What is missing is an Internet access that offers a decent level of privacy for average users out of the box. In this paper, we survey suitable lightweight anonymity solutions and present avenues for future research so that Internet service providers can offer anonymity online without compromising performance and usability, i.e. an effortless solution for customers.

1 Introduction

Surveillance is commonplace on the Internet. Not only intelligence services, but also corporate service providers are interested in the activities of users. Ubiquitous connectivity and pervasive data collection are increasing the size of our digital footprint. Mobile devices like smartphones, tablets, and other wearable devices allow more detailed profiling of user behaviour and preferences, resulting in severe infringements of privacy. The right to informational self-determination is becoming more and more difficult to enforce.

Policy makers are struggling to keep up with the fast-paced development. In the future, legislation may become unable to protect the right to informational self-determination, and users may completely lose control of their private data. Some citizens have already taken matters into their own hands. They use privacy tools as a means of self-defence.

Unfortunately, the currently available solutions for self-defence have not seen widespread adoption so far. According to the Tor Metrics project [37], the number of average Tor clients that connect to the Tor network per day from Germany is about 200,000 (based on data obtained in the last three months of 2015). Only a tiny fraction of the estimated 69 million [42] German Internet users route their traffic over the Tor network on a daily basis. Although the adoption of Tor has

J. Camenisch and D. Kesdoğan (Eds.): iNetSec 2015, LNCS 9591, pp. 82–94, 2016.
DOI: 10.1007/978-3-319-39028-4_7

increased since the Oxford Internet Institute carried out a similar analysis on a global level in 2013 [15]), Tor and other anonymisation systems like JAP are still far away from mainstream.

We believe that adoption of anonymity online will only increase if it causes (virtually) zero effort. Following the principle of privacy by design, anonymous Internet should be a available "out of the box" and not require any involvement of users. This paper surveys existing research on lightweight anonymity solutions that may be useful to turn this vision into a reality. Moreover, we summarise the most important challenges that should be addressed in future research.

The paper is organised as follows. In Sect. 2 we review the most important self-defence techniques that are available today, before we survey open issues and avenues for future research in Sect. 3. We conclude in Sect. 4.

2   State of the Art of Anonymity Online

In the following we review the most important tools that are used in practice at the moment.

Researchers have proposed a number of self-defence techniques. These efforts have resulted in tools such as Tor [27] and JAP [5] that encrypt and route the traffic of their users over multiple network nodes, providing relationship anonymity. Thus, the identity of users (their IP address, to be precise) is hidden from the destinations (for instance, the webservers) as well as observers on the network.

However, many users are switching from desktop computers to mobile and wearable devices, where the installation of client-side proxies or browser extensions is difficult or impossible. There *are* Tor clients for both Android and iOS, but their functionality is limited due to restrictions enforced by the operating systems. Apps like OnionBrowser for iOS [30] and Orbot for Android [31] can only anonymise their own traffic. Neither iOS nor Android offer users a straightforward way to route the traffic of all apps through an anonymisation network. Some apps try to work around these limitation, for instance by running a local proxy in the background or by intercepting traffic of other apps, which is usually only possible if the device has been rooted. However, these workarounds are hardly suitable for non-experts.

Recently, privacy activists have come up with dedicated network devices that can be plugged into the home network. Popular efforts are Anonabox [4], InvizBox [22], Safeplug [35], and eBlocker [8]. Typically, these designs consist of low-cost hardware running a Tor client. While such deployments improve usability, they also increase the attack surface (cf. Anonabox, which suffered from severe vulnerabilities [16]). Moreover, the utility of anonymising home network routers is limited. Users only benefit from them when they are at home, but not when they are on the road with their mobile devices. Furthermore, performance issues with the underlying anonymisation techniques are not addressed. Another open problem is the automatic and robust filtering of additional identifying information such as cookies, HTTP referrer, fingerprinting, or HTTP POST parameters (cf. Sect. 3.4). Nevertheless, anonymising home routers are in demand, as evidenced by successful crowd funding campaigns on Indiegogo and Kickstarter, some of them raising more than 100,000 Euro [24].

For many Internet users the main privacy concern is behavioural profiling, i.e. being tracked by third parties [28]. Over the past five years, a number of countermeasures have been released, either taking the form of browser add-ons or of stand-alone tools.

Ghostery [12] is a popular browser add-on for self-defence that blocks widespread advertising and tracking technologies embedded on websites. It is based on ad-hoc filtering techniques and a database. The embedded tracking snippets do not get blocked before the user approves, which allows for manual inspection and ensures compatibility. As a consequence, the user can balance the trade-off between anonymity, functionality, and usability.

A different approach at achieving the same goal has been studied and developed by the Electronic Frontier Foundation, resulting in a browser add-on called Privacy Badger [10]. The add-on prevents trackers from following user activities over several different websites and browsing sessions by keeping track of different tracking sources and content which is automatically loaded while surfing. Communication with servers is blocked as soon as their already loaded content appears to be used for tracking. The user gets visual feedback via green, yellow, or red slides. Furthermore, Privacy Badger maintains a so-called cookie-blocking yellowlist to identify and allow tracking activities, which are actually important for certain functionalities, while filtering of third-party cookies and referrers is still enforced.

Torres et al. have developed the browser extension FP-Block [38] to counter fingerprinting-based tracking. The authors motivate their work with the observation that Tor fails to meet the needs of ordinary users due to its poor usability. They argue that intra-domain tracking is an acceptable and sometimes even useful feature of web services, in contrast to cross-domain tracking, which reveals user behaviour and preferences not only to one specific website, but potentially globally over large portions of the Internet. Therefore, FP-Block creates and manages several different spoofed web identities as well as a set of fingerprintable browser characteristics, and presents those unrelated identities to different web domains.

ShareMeNot [34] focuses on preventing social media sites from tracking user behaviour and visited websites. To this end cookies relating to "share" widgets, which are embedded and automatically loaded in many websites, are automatically stripped from the HTTP traffic. The transit of these cookies is only allowed if a user wants to interact with them.

Solving the problem of being tracked or profiled by companies via advertisements, referrers, or other techniques that get activated during user clicks of browsing sessions is likewise targeted by the browser add-ons TrackMeNot [20] and AdNauseam [2]. In contrast to the aforementioned countermeasures, these tools utilise a dummy traffic approach to hide the attributable behaviour and preference of users, which is valuable information for tracking or advertising companies. TrackMeNot obfuscates requests to web search engines. It sends fake queries generated from lists of popular search queries as well as RSS feeds of popular news websites and then clicks on some of the search results to mimic typical user behaviour. AdNauseam automatically activates all advertisements blocked by an ad-blocker on all websites visited by a user, creating the impression that the user actually clicked these ads.

The demand for the mentioned add-ons seems to be high, although they can only be used with some browsers. However, a large part of the online activities nowadays include audio or video streaming as well as interactions on social networks that take place via dedicated (mobile) applications instead of a web browser. Furthermore, the wide range of browser-based countermeasures shows the many possibilities of being tracked and profiled by third parties. New tracking approaches, focusing on other environments like mobile platforms, will certainly be developed in the near future.

3 Avenues for Future Research

The reasons for the low adoption of tools that provide anonymity online are manifold. Figure 1 presents four typical user groups and what could be done so that they become anonymous online. Some citizens just do not care for privacy online (Groups 1 and 2). Others do care for privacy, but are not aware of the available anonymisation tools (Group 3). Citizens in Group 4 are privacy-conscious *and* aware of anonymisation tools, but do not use them. This irrational behaviour is due to psychological effects such as immediate gratification and hyperbolic discounting [1]. The violation of privacy is a risk that is difficult to grasp and the benefits of using an anonymisation network unfold in the distant future. The impact on comfort, on the other hand, is very tangible: First, there is some initial effort, i.e. users have to install (and also correctly configure) a dedicated client software or browser extension. Second, there is a loss of comfort, because they have to use a restricted web browser that breaks some web sites and surfing on the Internet is slower than before.

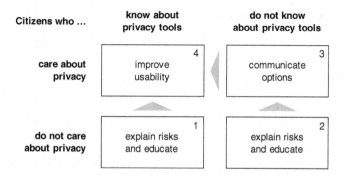

Fig. 1. Four approaches to increase the use of online anonymity solutions among different groups of citizens

Therefore, educating users and advertising the available anonymity solutions are insufficient. First, a certain fraction of users in Groups 1–3 cannot be reached by these efforts anyway, and second, eventually those who are susceptible to these efforts will eventually end up in Group 4, being frustrated by the limitations of existing anonymity solutions. Ordinary users are unlikely to accept dedicated anonymity tools until their usage becomes virtually effortless and comfortable.

In our view, effortless anonymity that does not compromise comfort is possible by moving towards network layer anonymisation and relaxing the attacker model.

Moving the anonymisation functionality from the transport layer (TCP overlay networks like Tor) *to the network layer* (IP-level anonymisation) decreases its overhead and avoids undesirable effects of TCP congestion control. In addition, this allows users of mobile devices to connect to the anonymisation service without any additional client software, because all of their IP traffic could be transparently routed over the anonymisation network. However, feasibility and security of this approach are unknown so far. Note that the current version of Tor also supports transparent forwarding of traffic, but it is restricted to TCP connections and DNS queries [39].

The second step towards zero-effort privacy protection consists in *relaxing the attacker model*, as proposed by Hsiao et al. [21]. Not all users need the protection offered by Tor and JAP. Some are willing to trust their local Internet Service Provider (ISP). They only want their identity – which can be revealed both by their IP address as well as other tracking mechanisms, such as cookies – to be concealed from the visited websites and third parties (such as ad networks). This more limited attacker model would make it possible to delegate anonymisation to the ISP, as proposed by Raghavan et al. [32]. Ideally, users would not have to install any client-side software or set up additional hardware at home.

Thus, zero-effort anonymity trades off perfect anonymity for better usability, i.e. our objective is to raise the overall level of anonymity that is available out of the box for the majority of users. Achieving this goal involves a number of challenges, which we will describe in the following.

3.1 Relationship Anonymity

The classical approach to provide anonymity for users consists in relaying traffic through multiple mixes or using onion routing. Both techniques achieve relationship anonymity between senders and receivers. Unfortunately, the currently available anonymity services introduce a relatively large overhead, both in terms of message size as well as latency. Moreover, the available bandwidth is limited. The effective performance cannot compete with typical DSL and cable broadband access, as has been shown to be the case for Tor by Fabian et al. [11]. Thus, the existing anonymity services are not suitable for applications that require near real-time transmission of messages (e.g. IP telephony) or a high bandwidth (e.g. video streaming or downloads).

The main goal is therefore to improve the efficiency of mixing and onion routing. This goal can be achieved in two ways: The first approach tries to tailor anonymity solutions to a specific application or protocol, as is the case for the EncDNS [18] service that relays encrypted DNS messages via DNS. The second approach consists in understanding and tuning the relationship between the underlying transport and the characteristics of the overlay network [40].

One possible direction consists in moving from application layer (such as JAP, which mainly anonymises HTTP traffic) and transport layer (such as Tor, which anonymises TCP traffic) overlays to *network layer* overlays in order to decrease the overhead. This would also eliminate performance issues introduced by the combination of TCP congestion control and multiplexing in the overlay such as *head-of-line blocking* and *cross-connection interference* [3,23,33].

LAP [21] is an example for this approach. It aims to achieve user anonymity by obscuring source and destination addresses via changes in path establishment during routing. HORNET, which was proposed by Chen et al. [7], is another concept aiming to provide anonymity "as an in-network service to all users". Dovetail [36] also strives to attain network-level security. Unlike LAP and HOR-NET, it fully replaces IP (while HORNET can build upon IP Segment Routing, it can also be used with replacement protocols). Both HORNET and Dovetail do not require a relaxation of the classical threat model and aim to protect users against all adversaries, including global adversaries and the ISP.

Ideally, all traffic should be routed through an anonymity network without the user having to manually configure the applications or the operating system to use the anonymity service. A system achieving this goal can be implemented in different ways.

On the one hand, the anonymity client software could be integrated into the user's router. This has the advantage of not requiring active support by the user's ISP (other than the ISP allowing their customers to use their own routers). Users are also not required to trust their ISPs, as providers would only see traffic flowing from a customer to the anonymisation network, but do not get to know the true destination and contents of the message. The disadvantage of a router-based solution is that it will be typically more expensive and less convenient for users due to the initial setup effort.

On the other hand, the responsibility for routing a user's traffic through an anonymisation network could also be delegated to the ISP. Such a design would require absolutely no effort from users. However, the provider has to explicitly support and offer this service, as such a change cannot be implemented by the user. Another problem is that this model requires users to trust their ISP, as the provider would be aware of the contents of all (not otherwise encrypted) messages as well as their source and destination.

3.2 Privacy-Preserving Assignment of IP Addresses

Relaying traffic over multiple mixes or onion routers hides the source IP address of a user from destination servers as well as from other observers on the network, i.e. it obscures the relationship between sources and destinations. Many ordinary users do not demand this rather high level of protection. Their main concern is that destination servers can track their (parallel or consecutive) activities in order

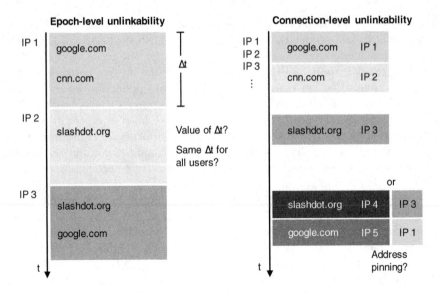

Fig. 2. Address assignment schemes for epoch- and connection-level unlinkability

to create behavioural profiles. So far, tracking mainly happens on the application layer, for instance via cookies (see Sect. 3.4), and not on the network layer.

However, in principle ad networks could also rely on the source IP addresses to track individual users over time, especially if these addresses change only rarely [6,43]. We expect IP-based tracking to become more relevant in the future due to the rising adoption of IPv6. In the following, we will outline lightweight approaches that specifically prevent IP-based tracking. These approaches are of interest for users who only want their activities to be *unlinkable* rather than hiding their source IP address altogether.

We believe that this could be achieved at very low cost if ISPs changed their address assignment schemes. Today, ISPs assign a single IP address (or IPv6 prefix) to each customer for a certain period of time. Typical addresses change after 24 h or whenever the broadband router goes offline and online again. In the following we describe two design alternatives for privacy-preserving address assignment and the challenges that have to be overcome (cf. also [17]). Figure 2 shows a side-by-side comparison.

First, ISPs could assign new IP addresses (or prefixes) much more frequently, i.e. resulting in epochs with a duration Δt of a few seconds or minutes. Implemented on its own, this approach provides *epoch-level unlinkability* of IP addresses, which limits the amount of information available for profiling. Obviously, Δt should be as short as possible, because all IP packets sent by a customer within an epoch originate from the same source IP address. Parallel activities and everything within an epoch can still be linked. Apart from determining suitable values for Δt, future research has to look into the feasibility of potential traffic analysis attacks: When a distinctive activity (such as browsing a rather unpopular website) or a set of activities span multiple epochs, it may be possible to link these events – and potentially all other activities within these epochs. This could be prevented by source address pinning, i.e. re-using the same source IP address that was used for sending traffic to a destination (identified by its IP address or domain name) for the first time. However, address pinning considerably complicates address space management for the ISP.

As an extension to the first scheme, ISPs could provide multiple randomly selected addresses or IPv6 prefixes from their address pool to a customer in each epoch. This would enable customers to make use of multiple source IP addresses at the same time, either one for each destination address or – in the extreme case – one for each TCP connection or even IP packet. This *connection-level unlinkability* would prevent websites and ad networks from linking requests based on IP addresses. However, assigning multiple addresses at once requires considerable changes to the network stack on routers of both the ISP and the customer, as well as to protocols such as DHCP and PPP. Furthermore, it is critical to evaluate the effects of changing source addresses in practice. Changing the source IP too often may cause compatibility problems: For security reasons some web applications terminate HTTP sessions (maintained using cookies) if the source IP address changes during a session. Such issues could be resolved by the aforementioned source address pinning as well. However, enabling address pinning for all destinations by default is undesirable, because it would allow the webservers of ad networks (whose web servers have constant destination addresses) to link requests of the same user.

Apart from the already mentioned assignment variants and strategies for address re-use, there is another more fundamental design choice regarding the role of the ISP: Do we request the ISP merely to provide all the means for preserving privacy, or do we trust the ISP so much that we delegate the actual task of preserving privacy to the ISP? In the first case, the role of the ISP is solely to assign a sufficient amount of addresses to the customer's router and the decision which address is used for an outgoing packet is made on the customer's premises. This offers tech-savvy customers control and transparency, but is technically challenging due to necessary changes to the authentication protocols between the router and the ISP. The second case would be much easier to implement. In fact, it could be implemented by the ISP on its own in a transparent fashion, for instance via carrier-grade network address translation (cf. Raghavan et al. [32]).

3.3 Privacy by Obfuscation

User privacy can also be ensured by obfuscating *activities* rather than identities. This is possible by generating plausible dummy requests and sending them along with the real requests of a user. If the fake requests resemble normal user activity closely enough, it is impossible for the server to distinguish them from the real requests initiated by the user.

TrackMeNot implements this approach to obfuscate queries to search engines. The more recently presented browser add-on AdNauseam aims to make user profiling for targeted advertising impossible by automatically "clicking" on every ad encountered during websurfing (cf. Sect. 2). Zhao et al. proposed a similar concept for DNS, referred to as "range queries" [44]. However, range queries have been shown to not obfuscate a user's surfing behaviour sufficiently, because the automatically generated dummy requests are not plausible [19]. Generating plausible dummy traffic is still an open problem.

Dummy traffic can either be generated by a software running on a user's client computer (or router) or by the ISP. Generating it on the premises of a user makes deployment cumbersome, not only for users but also for vendors: The dummy generator would need access to (individual or aggregated) traffic profiles of other users in order to create plausible dummies. Therefore, at first sight, delegating the generation of dummy traffic to the ISP is an intriguing idea. After all, the ISP has access to the traffic of all its customers. However, ISPs may be unwilling to offer such a feature, because they risk being sued by service providers that suffer from their dummy traffic.

Whether or not dummy traffic is a suitable tool to provide privacy is debatable. It challenges the dominant business model on the Internet that relies on revenues from advertisements. Moreover, it is a question of morality: Is it acceptable that individuals harm other parties and the environment in pursuit of their own privacy interests? After all, dummy traffic increases the burden on both the servers, which the dummy requests are being sent to, as well as the network infrastructure in general. Eventually, operators would have to invest in additional servers to respond to the dummy requests, which are of no use apart from cloaking user activities. In consequence, energy consumption and thus carbon emissions rise: If all search queries to Google were to be obfuscated by sending an extra ten dummy queries along with each genuine query, this would lead to an additional use of energy equivalent to an emission of about 1.85 million tonnes of carbon dioxide per year (assuming 1.2 trillion queries per year [14], 0.0003 kWh per query [13] and 515.735 grammes of carbon emissions per kWh generated in the US [41]).

3.4 Application Layer Issues

So far, we have discussed techniques to protect the identity of users on the network level (i.e. their IP address). On its own, none of these techniques is sufficient to protect anonymity in practice, because it is rendered ineffective if identifying pieces of information are present on other layers of the network stack, for instance on the transport (e.g. TCP timestamps [25]), session (e.g. TLS client certificates), or application layers. In this section we focus on the application layer.

A well-known example of this are HTTP cookies, whose purpose is to be able to re-identify a user upon subsequent visits to a website. However, re-identification of web users does not necessarily rely on explicit identifiers, but can also be performed in a more subtle way, such as via browser fingerprinting [9,29].

However, application layer tracking does not apply to web browsing only. For instance, some BitTorrent clients disclose the IP address of the client's machine in the handshake messages [26]. Anonymity is only maintained if all identifying pieces of information are filtered from transmitted messages. Automated filtering of identifying pieces of data is challenging for three reasons: First, the identifiers may take many different forms, which makes it difficult to locate them within the transferred data. Strategic adversaries could even set up a subtle side-channel to bypass the filter. Second, the filter has to replace the identifying pieces of data in a syntactically and semantically correct way so that the functionality of the application is not impaired. Third, the filter must be able to differentiate between unintentionally transferred identifiers and intentional linkage, for instance for the purpose of maintaining state with session cookies during online shopping.

Further, there is the question of placement of such a filter. In order to minimise effort for users, it would be desirable to place the filter at the ISP side. As in routing traffic through anonymisation networks (as described in Sect. 3.1), placing responsibility with the ISP requires users to trust their ISP. However, such a setup is ineffective here, because identifiers in encrypted streams (including very commonly used HTTPS connections) would pass the filter unaltered. Users would have to install a root certificate issued by their ISP in order to enable the ISP to filter identifiers in encrypted traffic. However, this comes at the cost of losing end-to-end security, which makes it a very poor trade-off.

As an alternative, the traffic could be filtered on the user's side, for instance directly on each of the user's devices. In contrast to deployment at the ISP, this solution is more cumbersome, because users would have to install plug-ins for their applications or – if this is not possible – explicitly configure them to send the traffic through the filtering tool. Effort for the user could be decreased by deploying the filter on the user's router, analogous to the concepts described in Sect. 3.1. Regardless of the concrete placement, users would still have to install a trusted root certificate on their devices for the inspection of encrypted connections. If this certificate was generated and stored only on the premises of the user, end-to-end security would be intact (under the assumption that the vendor of the filter cannot access the private key).

3.5 Policy Issues

In many countries, data retention legislation is in place to enable law enforcement to combat cyber crime. Typically, this kind of legislation requires ISPs to retain certain data for a set period of time, most importantly which IP address a customer was assigned at what time.

If the responsibility for anonymising a customer's traffic is transferred to the ISP, the ISP may be in conflict with such legislation, which would effectively prevent the implementation of ISP-based anonymisation services. Therefore, it needs to be ensured that the provider can still abide the law by retaining all information required. Depending on the interpretation of the law, this may require ISPs to store the outward-facing IP address(es), i.e. the one of the exit node, and all internal identifiers required to trace back the traffic to a particular customer. Efficient storage techniques will have to be employed to cope with the resulting amount of data.

3.6   Verifiability by End Users

A zero-effort anonymisation solution that is active out of the box should ideally not interfere with the user experience at all. However, good usability has its price: Users would not notice if their traffic was *not* routed through the anonymisation system, either due to unintentional system failures or malicious activity.

One approach to solving this problem consists in a website that checks what kind of information it can get about a user. While such an *anonymity self assessment* is simple to set up, it must be visited by users manually. Moreover, the site has to be trusted by users to show correct results and it might be difficult to determine whether the IP address the webserver sees actually belongs to the user's computer or to a server within the anonymisation network.

Another approach would be a client-side *watchdog software* that continuously checks whether IP anonymisation works properly. The watchdog, which would have to be installed by users on their devices, would automate the process of manually visiting a self-assessment website by contacting one or multiple (trustworthy) remote servers. In case of hardware-based anonymity systems, this could be implemented on the customer's network router that notifies its owner via a status indicator LED.

4   Conclusion

Since the extensive surveillance capabilities of security agencies have been revealed, many citizens have lost faith in technological solutions for privacy protection. As a result, some users have fallen into a state of apathy. They are unwilling to concern themselves with privacy tools for self-defence at all. On the other hand, users who want to protect their privacy have to make difficult decisions that impede both usability and performance, causing analysis paralysis.

In order to change the state of affairs, we believe that it is worthwhile to pursue the goal of designing zero-effort privacy solutions. In this paper we have reviewed existing ideas and presented a number of areas for future work that are based on relaxing the attacker model, network-level anonymization, privacy-preserving IP address assignment, and privacy via obfuscation of activities. Deploying them in practice would raise the overall level of anonymity available out of the box for the majority of users.

References

1. Acquisti, A.: Privacy in electronic commerce and the economics of immediate gratification. In: Proceedings of the 5th ACM Conference on Electronic Commerce, EC 2004, pp. 21–29. ACM, New York (2004)
2. AdNauseam (2015). https://dhowe.github.io/AdNauseam/
3. AlSabah, M., Goldberg, I.: PCTCP: per-circuit TCP-over-IPsec transport for anonymous communication overlay networks. In: Sadeghi, A.R., Gligor, V.D., Yung, M. (eds.) Conference on Computer and Communications Security (CCS 2013), pp. 349–360. ACM (2013)

4. Anonabox (2015). https://www.anonabox.com
5. Berthold, O., Federrath, H., Köpsell, S.: Web MIXes: a system for anonymous and unobservable internet access. In: Federrath, H. (ed.) Designing Privacy Enhancing Technologies. LNCS, vol. 2009, pp. 115–129. Springer, Heidelberg (2001)
6. Casado, M., Freedman, M.J.: Peering through the shroud: the effect of edge opacity on IP-based client identification. In: Proceedings of 4th Symposium on Networked Systems Design and Implementation (NSDI 2007), Cambridge, Massachusetts, USA. USENIX, 11–13 April 2007
7. Chen, C., Asoni, D.E., Barrera, D., Danezis, G., Perrig, A.: HORNET: high-speed onion routing at the network layer. In: Ray, I., Li, N., Kruegel, C. (eds.) Proceedings of the 22nd ACM SIGSAC Conference on Computer and Communications Security, Denver, CO, USA, pp. 1441–1454. ACM, 12–16 October 2015
8. eBlocker (2015). https://www.eblocker.com/
9. Eckersley, P.: How unique is your web browser? In: Atallah, M.J., Hopper, N.J. (eds.) PETS 2010. LNCS, vol. 6205, pp. 1–18. Springer, Heidelberg (2010)
10. Electronic Frontier Foundation: Privacy Badger (2015). https://www.eff.org/privacybadger
11. Fabian, B., Goertz, F., Kunz, S., Müller, S., Nitzsche, M.: Privately waiting - a usability analysis of the Tor anonymity network. In: Santana, M., Luftman, J.N., Vinze, A.S. (eds.) 16th Americas Conference on Information Systems, AMCIS 2010, Lima, Peru. Association for Information Systems, 12–15 August 2010
12. Ghostery (2015). https://www.ghostery.com/en/
13. Google Official Blog: Powering a google search (2009). https://googleblog.blogspot.de/2009/01/powering-google-search.html
14. Google Zeitgeist (2012). https://www.google.com/zeitgeist/2012/#the-world
15. Graham, M., De Sabbata, S.: Information Geographies at the Oxford Internet Institute The anonymous Internet (2015). http://geography.oii.ox.ac.uk/?page=tor
16. Greenberg, A.: Anonabox Recalls 350 "Privacy" Routers for Security Flaws (2015). http://www.wired.com/2015/04/anonabox-recall/
17. Herrmann, D., Arndt, C., Federrath, H.: IPv6 prefix alteration: an opportunity to improve online privacy. In: Proceedings of 1st Workshop on Privacy and Data Protection Technology (PDPT 2012), Co-located with Amsterdam Privacy Conference (APC 2012), Amsterdam, Netherlands, 7–10 October 2012. http://arxiv.org/abs/1211.4704
18. Herrmann, D., Fuchs, K.-P., Lindemann, J., Federrath, H.: EncDNS: a lightweight privacy-preserving name resolution service. In: Kutyłowski, M., Vaidya, J. (eds.) ICAIS 2014, Part I. LNCS, vol. 8712, pp. 37–55. Springer, Heidelberg (2014)
19. Herrmann, D., Maaß, M., Federrath, H.: Evaluating the security of a DNS query obfuscation scheme for private web surfing. In: Cuppens, F., Jajodia, S., Abou El Kalam, A., Sans, T., Cuppens-Boulahia, N. (eds.) SEC 2014. IFIP AICT, vol. 428, pp. 205–219. Springer, Heidelberg (2014)
20. Howe, D.C., Nissenbaum, H.: TrackMeNot: resisting surveillance in web search. In: Lessons from the Identity Trail: Anonymity, Privacy, and Identity in a Networked Society, pp. 417–436 (2009)
21. Hsiao, H.C., Kim, T.J., Perrig, A., Yamada, A., Nelson, S.C., Gruteser, M., Meng, W.: LAP: lightweight anonymity and privacy. In: 2012 IEEE Symposium on Security and Privacy (SP), pp. 506–520. IEEE (2012)
22. InvizBox (2015). https://www.invizbox.io/
23. Karol, M., Hluchyj, M., Morgan, S.: Input versus output queueing on a space-division packet switch. IEEE Trans. Commun. **35**(12), 1347–1356 (1987)

24. Kickstarter: InvizBox Go - Privacy Made Easy (2015). https://www.kickstarter. com/projects/683682172/invizbox-go
25. Kohno, T., Broido, A., Claffy, K.C.: Remote physical device fingerprintin. IEEE Trans. Dependable Sec. Comput. **2**(2), 93–108 (2005)
26. Manils, P., Abdelberi, C., Blond, S.L., Kâafar, M.A., Castelluccia, C., Legout, A., Dabbous, W.: Compromising Tor anonymity exploiting P2P information leakage. CoRR abs/1004.1461 (2010). http://arxiv.org/abs/1004.1461
27. Mathewson, N., Syverson, P., Dingledine, R.: Tor: the second-generation onion router. In: The Proceedings of the 13th USENIX Security Symposium (2004)
28. Mayer, J.R., Mitchell, J.C.: Third-party web tracking: policy and technology. In: IEEE Symposium on Security and Privacy, SP 2012, San Francisco, California, USA, pp. 413–427. IEEE Computer Society, 21–23 May 2012
29. Mowery, K., Shacham, H.: Pixel perfect: fingerprinting canvas in HTML5. In: Proceedings of Web 2.0 Security and Privacy (2012)
30. OnionBrowser iOS App (2015). https://mike.tig.as/onionbrowser/
31. Orbot Android App (2015). https://guardianproject.info/apps/orbot/
32. Raghavan, B., Kohno, T., Snoeren, A.C., Wetherall, D.: Enlisting ISPs to improve online privacy: IP address mixing by default. In: Goldberg, I., Atallah, M.J. (eds.) PETS 2009. LNCS, vol. 5672, pp. 143–163. Springer, Heidelberg (2009)
33. Reardon, J., Goldberg, I.: Improving Tor using a TCP-over-DTLS tunnel. In: USENIX Security Symposium, pp. 119–134. USENIX Association (2009)
34. Roesner, F., Kohno, T., Wetherall, D.: Detecting and defending against third-party tracking on the web. In: Proceedings of the 9th USENIX Conference on Networked Systems Design and Implementation, NSDI 2012, p. 12, USENIX Association, Berkeley, CA, USA (2012)
35. Safeplug (2015). https://pogoplug.com/safeplug
36. Sankey, J., Wright, M.: Dovetail: stronger anonymity in next-generation internet routing. In: De Cristofaro, E., Murdoch, S.J. (eds.) PETS 2014. LNCS, vol. 8555, pp. 283–303. Springer, Heidelberg (2014)
37. TorMetrics: Top-10 countries by directly connecting users (2015). https://metrics. torproject.org/userstats-relay-table.html
38. Torres, C.F., Jonker, H., Mauw, S.: FP-Block: usable web privacy by controlling browser fingerprinting. In: Pernul, G., Y A Ryan, P., Weippl, E. (eds.) ESORICS. LNCS, vol. 9327, pp. 3–19. Springer, Heidelberg (2015). doi:10.1007/978-3-319-24177-7_1
39. Tor Trac Wiki: Transparently Routing Traffic Through Tor (2015). https://trac. torproject.org/projects/tor/wiki/doc/TransparentProxy
40. Tschorsch, F., Scheuermann, B.: How (not) to build a transport layer for anonymity overlays. ACM SIGMETRICS Perform. Eval. Rev. **40**(4), 101–106 (2013)
41. United States Environmental Protection Agency: Power profiler (2015). http://www2.epa.gov/energy/power-profiler
42. Worldbank Open Data (2015). http://data.worldbank.org/
43. Xie, Y., Yu, F., Achan, K., Gillum, E., Goldszmidt, M., Wobber, T.: How dynamic are IP addresses? In: Proceedings of Conference on Applications, Technologies, Architectures, and Protocols for Computer Communications (SIGCOMM 2007), pp. 301–312. ACM, New York (2007)
44. Zhao, F., Hori, Y., Sakurai, K.: Analysis of privacy disclosure in DNS query. In: 2007 International Conference on Multimedia and Ubiquitous Engineering (MUE 2007), Seoul, Korea, pp. 952–957. IEEE Computer Society, 26–28 April 2007

Cryptography

Reviving the Idea of Incremental Cryptography for the Zettabyte Era Use Case: Incremental Hash Functions Based on SHA-3

Hristina Mihajloska[1(✉)], Danilo Gligoroski[2], and Simona Samardjiska[1]

[1] Faculty of Computer Science and Engineering, UKIM, Skopje, Macedonia
{hristina.mihajloska,simona.samardjiska}@finki.ukim.mk
[2] Department of Telematics, NTNU, Trondheim, Norway
danilog@item.ntnu.no

Abstract. According to several recent studies, the global IP communication and digital storage have already surpassed the zettabyte threshold (10^{21} bytes). The Internet entered the zettabyte era in which fast and secure computations are important more than ever. One solution for certain types of computations, that may offer a speedup up to several orders of magnitude, is the incremental cryptography. While the idea of incremental crypto primitives is not new, so far its potential has not been fully exploited. In this paper, we define two incremental hash functions iSHAKE128 and iSHAKE256 based on the recent NIST proposal for SHA-3 Extendable-Output Functions SHAKE128 and SHAKE256. We describe two practical implementation scenarios of the newly introduced hash functions and compare them with the already known tree-based hash scheme. We show the trends of efficiency gains as the amount of data increases in comparison to the standard tree-based incremental schemes. Our proposals iSHAKE128 and iSHAKE256 provide security against collision attacks of 128 and 256 bits, respectively.

Keywords: Incremental hashing · SHA-3 · SHAKE128 · SHAKE256 · iSHAKE128 · iSHAKE256 · Zettabyte era

1 Introduction

The idea of incremental hashing was introduced by Bellare, Goldreich and Goldwasser in [4] and improved later in [5]. Incremental hashing can be achieved also by using Merkle trees [15] as it is discussed for example in [7]. In a nutshell, the idea of incremental hashing is that if we have already computed the hash value of some document, and this document is modified in one part, then instead of re-computing the hash value of the whole document from scratch, we just need to update it, performing computations only on the changed part of the document. In this way, incremental hashing of closely related documents, compared to classical hashing, offers speed gain up to several orders of magnitude. Yet, so far, the concept has not been particularly well accepted by the community nor

© IFIP International Federation for Information Processing
Published by Springer International Publishing Switzerland 2016. All Rights Reserved
J. Camenisch and D. Kesdoğan (Eds.): iNetSec 2015, LNCS 9591, pp. 97–111, 2016.
DOI: 10.1007/978-3-319-39028-4_8

the industry, and this is mainly due to the following two reasons: 1. The security level of the incremental hash functions of Bellare et al. [4,5] is detached from the size of the produced hash value, since a standard security of 128 bits requires outputs of several thousand bits. This is very different from the ordinary cryptographic hash functions such as SHA-1, SHA-2, SHA-3, where the size of the hash value corresponds to the claimed bit-security level of the hash function. 2. The implementations of these hash functions require expensive modular operations over large prime integers, which makes them one or more orders of magnitude slower than the ordinary cryptographic hash functions.

In the meantime the size of the digital universe has already surpassed 4.4 zettabytes and the projections are that by 2020, it will reach 44 zettabytes [10]. In another report, the Cisco Visual Networking Index [9] predicted that "the annual global IP traffic will pass the zettabyte threshold by the end of 2015, and will reach 1.4 zettabytes per year by 2017." Additionally, the data storage cost according to the latest reports is no longer an issue (see [3]). Hence, the sheer scale of data mentioned, already calls for new solutions that will use the paradigm of incrementality.

Let us consider the use case scenario of sensor networks where data comes from the nodes whose data rates rapidly increase as sensor technology improves and as the number of sensors expands [12]. A typical representative for this scenario is environmental sensor networks used for natural disaster prevention or weather forecasting. In these cases, all data that is collected from different sensors should be publicly available, with data integrity guaranteed by digital signatures from a trusted party. Thus, data hashing is unavoidable, and as the dataset is being updated, the hash value should be recomputed. Normally, the update of such datasets is done by appending new data or by changing a small part of the existing dataset. As the size of the dataset grows, (and can reach hundreds of terabytes [18]), recalculating the hash value of the entire dataset can become notoriously demanding in terms of both time and energy. An incremental update, on the other hand, can reduce the recalculation of the hash value to the minimum, and only of the parts of the dataset that have changed, or have been appended.

Another use case scenario where updates come in the form of insertions of new elements or modifications of existing data are distributed storage systems for managing structured data, such as Cloud Bigtable by Google [8]. It is designed to scale to a very large size, like petabytes of data across thousands of commodity servers. Its data model uses Google *SSTable* file format to internally store data. Each SSTable contains a sequence of blocks typically of 64 KB in size and every block has its own unique index that is used to locate the block. Using this kind of file formats where blocks have its unique numbers, incremental hashing can be successfully implemented despite the variable-size setting: In addition to the update operation, in order to perform incremental hash calculations, additional insert and delete operations should be introduced.

The trade-off between re-hashing and incremental hashing is simply in the storing of additional data overhead in order to get computation speed. Instead of rehashing the whole file (for example 1 GB), with the incremental hashing you just need to re-hash a small part of it (for example 1 MB), but the price is to keep a data overhead used in the process of incremental hashing.

The initial idea for an incremental hash function based on the recent NIST proposal for SHA-3, Extendable-Output Functions SHAKE128 and SHAKE256 [17] was presented at the NIST SHA-3 2014 Workshop [11]. We improve that proposal, define two practical implementation instances: iSHAKE-128 and iSHAKE-256 and compare them with already known incremental tree-based hash schemes.

The paper is organized as follows: In Sect. 2 we give mathematical preliminaries and definitions about incremental hash functions. In Sect. 3 we give an algorithmic description of incremental operations for two practical settings. After that, in Sect. 4, we define two incremental hash functions with security levels of 128 and 256 bits. Comparison analysis between our proposals and incremental tree-based hash scheme is given in Sect. 5. Finally, we conclude our paper in Sect. 6 with recommendations on where and how to use our incremental hash functions.

2 Mathematical Preliminaries

2.1 Incremental Hash Functions

We will use the following definition for an incremental hash function adapted from [5, Sect. 3.1]:

Definition 1. *Let $h : \{0,1\}^b \to \{0,1\}^k$ be a compression function that maps b bits into k bits. Let the message M be represented as a concatenation of n blocks, where $n < N$ for some predefined number N which is larger than the number of blocks in any message we plan to hash, i.e., $M = M_1 \| M_2 \| \ldots \| M_n$. The size of each block M_i is determined by the following relation: $|M_i| = b - Length(ID_i)$, where ID_i is a unique identifier for the block M_i.*

For each block M_i, $i = 1, \ldots, n$, append ID_i to get an augmented block $\overline{M_i} = M_i \| ID_i$. For each $i = 1, \ldots, n$, apply h to $\overline{M_i}$ to get a hash value $y_i = h(\overline{M_i})$. Let $(G, \odot)$ be a commutative group with operation $\odot$ where $G \subseteq \{0,1\}^k$. Combine $y_1, \ldots, y_n$ via a combining group operation $\odot$ to get the final hash value

$$y = y_1 \odot y_2 \odot \ldots \odot y_n.$$

Denote the incremental hash function as:

$$y(M) = \mathrm{HASH}^h_{(G)}(M_1 \| M_2 \| \ldots \| M_n) = \bigodot_{i=1}^{n} h(M_i \| ID_i) \qquad (1)$$

Since the group $(G, \odot)$ is commutative, the computation is parallelizable too. In such a case, the combining group operation $\odot$ is commutative and invertible, and increments are done as follows. If block M_i changes to M'_i, then the new hash value is computed as $y(M') = y(M) \odot^{-1} h(\overline{M_i}) \odot h(\overline{M_i'})$ where $\odot^{-1}$ denotes the inverse operation in the group $(G, \odot)$ and $y(M)$ is the old hash value. The cost of an increment operation is two hash computations and two operations in G.

The choice of good combining operation is important for both security and efficiency. In [5] there are four different hash function families depending on the combining operation. In XHASH, the combining operation is bitwise XOR. The multiplicative hash, MuHASH uses multiplication in a group where the discrete logarithm problem is hard. AdHASH stands for hash function obtained by setting the combining operation to addition modulo a sufficiently large integer, and LtHASH uses vector addition. Out of these four, the scheme XHASH is not secure. The authors of [5] estimated that the hash value of size ≈ 1024 bits would suffice for the security level of 2^{80}. However, Wagner in [19] showed that using a generalized birthday attack, these parameters are breakable, implying that the size of the hash values should be much bigger (for standard security levels, even up to tens of thousands of bits). Wagner also showed how to solve the n-sum problem for certain operations (a special case of the balance problem), with time and space complexity of $O(n \cdot 2^{\frac{k}{1+\lg\lceil n\rceil}})$ using lists of size $2^{\frac{k}{1+\lg\lceil n\rceil}}$ elements. More precisely, Wagner [19] showed the following:

Proposition 1. *Let* $\mathrm{HASH}^h_{\langle G\rangle}$ *be an incremental hash function defined by Definition 1. For any* $Y \in \{0,1\}^k$ *the complexity of finding a preimage message* $M = M_1 \,\|\, M_2 \,\|\, \ldots \,\|\, M_n$ *of length* $n \leqslant N$ *blocks such that* $Y = \mathrm{HASH}^h_{\langle G\rangle}(M)$ *is:*

$$\min_{n\leqslant N} O(n \cdot 2^{\frac{k}{1+\lg\lceil n\rceil}}) \tag{2}$$

If the length of the messages is not restricted, then the minimum in Eq. (2) is achieved for messages of $n = 2^{\sqrt{k}-1}$ *blocks.*

So, 10–15 years ago, the lack of an urgent need to hash extremely big files, as well as the difference between the hash sizes of classical hash functions (160–512 bits) versus the hash sizes in the incremental case (2500–16000 bits due to Wagner's result [19]), killed the attractiveness of the concept of incremental hashing. However, there are new trends and a new reality. In particular: the latest SHA-3 standard allows arbitrary hash sizes [17]; the need for incremental digesting of big files is increasing and the cost of storing longer hash values is decreasing. These are the main reasons why we revive the idea of incremental hashing in this paper.

3   Incremental Hashing Scheme

We will instantiate the incremental hash function from Definition 1 in two practical settings: fixed-size data and variable-sized data. In the fixed-size data setting, the data that needs to be hashed has a predetermined fixed size, and thus the total number of data blocks is fixed. The real use case scenarios can be found in cloud services (Images of Virtual Machines [1,2], cloud storage [13]), digital movies distributions [16], collecting data from sensor networks and many more. In the fixed-size data scenario, the incremental operations that need to be implemented are: block replacement (*replace* operation) and block appending. The other setting is a variable-size data, such as managing structured data, where additionally the incremental operations for insertion (*insert* operation) and deletion (*delete* operation) of a block should be supported. In order to implement these operations, we will use dynamic data structures.

For both of the aforementioned scenarios, the basic algorithmic description is given in Algorithm 1. The underlying hash primitive and combining operation in the algorithm are the following:

Underlying Hash Function. The concrete hash function h has to map b bits into k bits (k is a multiple of 64), $h : \{0,1\}^b \rightarrow \{0,1\}^k$. Typical cryptographic hash functions such as SHA-1 or SHA-2 output a short hash value of 160 or 256 or 512 bits. However, for achieving security levels of 128 or 256 bits we need the value of k to be more than 2000 bits. We use the recently proposed Extendable-Output Functions SHAKE128 and SHAKE256 defined in the NIST Draft FIPS-202 [17]. Definition and security analysis are given in Sect. 4.

Combining Operation. For the compression function $h : \{0,1\}^b \rightarrow \{0,1\}^k$ where k is a multiple of 64 bits i.e. $k = 64 \cdot L$, we use word-wise addition in the commutative group $((\mathbb{Z}_{2^{64}})^{k/64}, \boxplus_{64})$, since it is a very efficient operation on the modern 64-bit CPUs. The operation $\boxplus_{64}$ represents 64-bit word-wise addition of $k/64$ words, and $\boxminus_{64}$ the inverse operation of word-wise subtraction of $k/64$ words (Fig. 1).

Using appropriate parameter values for the formulations above, we have two practical settings:

Algorithm 1 - Incremental hash function
Input. A sequence of blocks $M_1, M_2, \ldots, M_n$, where each M_i has a fixed size of $b - \mathrm{Length}(ID)$ bits.
Output. k bits of hash output.
1. For each block M_i, $i = 1, \ldots, n$, append ID_i to get an augmented block $\overline{M_i} = M_i \| ID_i$;   2. For each $i = 1, \ldots, n$, apply h to the blocks $\overline{M_i}$ to get a hash value $y_i = h(\overline{M_i})$;   3. Combine $y_1, \ldots, y_n$ via the group operation $\boxplus_{64}$ to get the final hash value: $$y = y_1 \boxplus_{64} y_2 \boxplus_{64} \cdots \boxplus_{64} y_n.$$ 4. Output y and store it.

Fig. 1. An algorithm for incremental hash function. Note that when we deal with the fixed size data $ID_i \equiv \langle i \rangle$ and for variable size setting it is $ID_i \equiv (BN_i, ptr_{BN_i})$

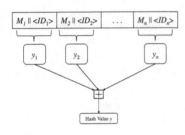

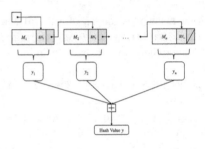

Fig. 2. Construction of incremental hash function for fixed size data.

Fig. 3. Construction of incremental hash function for variable size data. The colored parts present the data overhead. (Color figure online)

Algorithm 2 - Block Substitution
Input. The old block M_i and the new one M_i'.   The old hash value y.
Output. k bits of updated hash output.
1. Calculate $y_i = h(\overline{M_i})$;   2. Calculate $y_i' = h(\overline{M_i'})$;   3. Combine y, y_i and y_i' via a combining group operation $\boxplus_{64}$ to get the new updated final hash value $y' = y \boxminus_{64} y_i \boxplus_{64} y_i'$;   4. Output y' and store it.

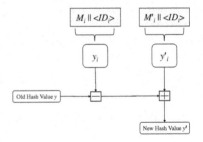

Fig. 4. An algorithm for incremental hash update operation: Block substitution.

Fig. 5. An update hash operation: Block substitution. Note that when we deal with the fixed data size $ID_i \equiv \langle i \rangle$ and for variable data size it is $ID_i \equiv (BN_i, ptr_{BN_{i+1}})$.

1. **Fixed-Size Data.** Hashing data which has a predetermine fixed size. The total number of data blocks is fixed, or can be changed by appending new blocks.

    Block Indexing. The data M is virtually divided into a fixed number of blocks $M_1, \ldots, M_n$. In this case, each block M_i has index i and its 64-bit binary encoding represents its unique identifier $ID_i \equiv \langle i \rangle$. This virtual division of data is shown in Fig. 2.

Incremental Update Operation. Once the hash function is applied on M, there is no need to repeat the same procedure for the whole M, but we can apply an incremental update operation. In this case the only update operation is the following one:

  – *Block Substitution.* This kind of update operation is applied on blocks M_i and M_i', where M_i' is the changed version of the block M_i. In total two block hash operations are applied. The hash update operation is given by Algorithm 2, and its graphical presentation in Fig. 5.

Data Overhead. There is no data overhead in this case. The final hash value has a size of k bits. This is the only data necessary to store if we want to recompute the hash.

2. **Variable-Size Data.** Hashing structured data which can have a variable size but where the data blocks always have a unique block identifier that does not change (Fig. 4).

Block Indexing. Data is divided into an ordered sequence of blocks $M_1, M_2, \ldots, M_n$. In this case the unique identifier consists of a nonce for that block, denoted as BN and a pointer to the nonce of the next block i.e. $ID_i \equiv (BN_i, ptr_{BN_{i+1}})$. Additionally, we need a head for this data structure i.e., a pointer for the first data block M_1 and the pointer of the last block M_n, that points to NULL i.e. $ptr_{BN_{n+1}} = \text{NULL}$. This hybrid data structure is, in fact, a singly-linked list with direct access via unique nonces and it is shown in Fig. 3.

Incremental Update Operations. In this case, we have the following three update operations:

  – *Block Substitution.* This kind of update operation is applied on block M_i and M_i' (the changed version of the block M_i). The hash update operation is the same as in the case of fixed size data settings, just with a difference in the presentation of ID, i.e. $ID_i = (BN_i, ptr_{BN_{i+1}})$. In total two block hash operations are applied. An algorithm is given by Algorithm 2 and its graphical presentation is given in Fig. 5.

  – *Block Insertion.* An insertion of a new block M_j with nonce BN_j after block M_i is performed by changing the unique identifier ID_i. The old value of $ID_i = (BN_i, ptr_{BN_{i+1}})$ is replaced by the new value $ID_i = (BN_i, ptr_{BN_j})$. In total three block hash operations are applied. This operation is given by Algorithm 3, and its graphical presentation in Fig. 8.

  – *Block Deletion.* To delete a block M_i we need to change the unique identifier of the $i-1$-th block, $ID_{i-1} = (BN_{i-1}, ptr_{BN_i})$ into $ID_{i-1} = (BN_{i-1}, ptr_{BN_{i+1}})$. In total three block hash operations are applied. The hash update operation is given by Algorithm 4, and its graphical presentation in Fig. 9.

Data Overhead. In this case, we have two sub-cases: (1): The size of the data that is hashed is tightly coupled with the media where it is stored. There is no data overhead, and the output is just k bits of the final hash value. (2): The size of the data that is hashed is flexible. The data

Algorithm 3 - Block Insertion	Algorithm 4 - Block Deletion
Input. The block M_i and ID_i after which the insertion will be done; The new block M_j;	**Input.** The block M_i and ID_i that should be deleted; The previous block M_{i-1} and ID_{i-1} from the sequence;
Output. k bits of hash output.	**Output.** k bits of hash output.
1. Calculate $y_i = h(\overline{M_i})$;	1. Calculate $y_{i-1} = h(\overline{M_{i-1}})$;
2. Calculate $y_j = h(\overline{M_j})$;	2. Calculate $y_i = h(\overline{M_i})$;
3. Transform ID_i into ID'_i i.e. $ID'_i \equiv (BN_i, ptr_{BN_j})$;	3. Transform ID_{i-1} into ID'_{i-1} as $ID'_{i-1} \equiv (BN_{i-1}, ptr_{BN_{i+1}})$;
4. Calculate $y'_i = h(\overline{M'_i})$, where $\overline{M'_i} = M_i \| ID'_i$;	4. Calculate $y'_{i-1} = h(\overline{M'_{i-1}})$, where $\overline{M'_{i-1}} = M_{i-1} \| (BN_{i-1}, ptr_{BN_{i+1}})$;
5. Combine y, y_i, y_j and y'_i via a combining group operation $\boxplus_{64}$ to get the new updated final hash value $y' = y \boxminus_{64} y_i \boxplus_{64} y'_i \boxplus_{64} y_j$;	5. Combine y, y_{i-1}, y_i and y'_{i-1} via a combining group operation $\boxplus_{64}$ to get the new updated final hash value $y' = y \boxminus_{64} y_{i-1} \boxminus_{64} y_i \boxplus_{64} y'_{i-1}$;
4. Output y and store it.	4. Output y and store it.

Fig. 6. An algorithm for incremental hash update operation in the variable size setting: Block insertion. Here the block M_j is inserted after the block M_i.

Fig. 7. An algorithm for incremental hash update operation in the variable size setting: Block deletion. Here the block M_i is deleted.

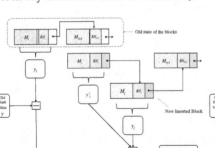

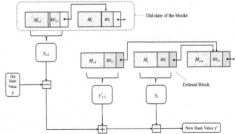

Fig. 8. An update hash operation: Block insertion. Here the block M_j is inserted after the block M_i.

Fig. 9. An update hash operation: Block deletion. Here the block M_i is deleted.

overhead is the information about the hybrid singly-linked list with direct access $ID_1, ID_2, \ldots, ID_n$ that is given together with the final hash value of size k bits (Fig. 6).

3.1   Incremental Tree Based Hash Scheme

Merkle proposed the tree hashing which can be used for incremental hashing [15]. In his scheme, the incrementality is implemented at the cost of storing all intermediate hash values of all tree levels. This can significantly increase the data

Algorithm 5 - One level tree hashing	**Algorithm 6 - Block substitution in tree hashing**
Input. A sequence of blocks $M_1, M_2, \ldots, M_n$ with fixed size of b bits.	**Input.** The position i of the old block and the new one M_i'. The old hash value y and all intermediate leaves hashes $y_1, y_2, \ldots, y_n$.
Output. $n * k$ bits of leaves hashes and k bits of the root hash.	**Output.** $n * k$ bits of leaves hashes and k bits of the root hash.
1. For each block $M_i, i = 1, \ldots, n$, apply h to them to get a hash value $y_i = h(M_i)$; 2. Concatenate $y_1, \ldots, y_n$ and apply h to the concatenated string to get the root hash value $$y = h(y_1 \| y_2, \ldots, y_n).$$ 3. Output y and store it. Store all the intermediate leaves hashes $y_1, y_2, \ldots, y_n$.	1. Calculate $y_i' = h(M_i')$; 2. Replace y_i with y_i'; 3. Concatenate $y_1, \ldots, y_n$ and apply h to the concatenated string to get the root hash value $y = h(y_1 \| y_2, \ldots, y_n)$. 4. Output y and store it. Store all the intermediate leaves hashes $y_1, y_2, \ldots, y_n$.

Fig. 10. An algorithm for incremental tree based hash function with depth 1.

Fig. 11. An algorithm for incremental tree based hash update operation: Block substitution.

overhead. To reduce the data overhead we can limit the tree depth to one or two leves [6,7]. Assume for simplicity that the hash tree has depth 1. The graphical representation of the one level tree hashing mode is given in Fig. 12. An algorithmic description of the one level tree hashing is given by Algorithm 5 (Fig. 7).

For this scheme, the data M is divided into blocks $M_1, M_2, \ldots, M_n$ and we need the following components:

1. **One Level Tree-Based Hash Function.** Any cryptographic hash function h that maps data with arbitrary size into k bits can be used. It has two stages:
   - *Hashing Tree Leaves.* The hash function h maps the leaves M_i of b bits into k bits i.e. $y_i = h(M_i)$.
   - *Root Hash.* The final hash value y is computed by hashing the concatenation of the hashes of the leaves, i.e. $y = h(y_1 \| y_2 \| \ldots \| y_n)$ (Fig. 10).
2. **Incremental Update Operation.** Once the root hash is computed, the update operation has the following variants:
   - *Block Substitution.* This kind of update operation is applied on blocks M_i and M_i', where M_i' is a changed version of the block M_i. In total one block hash operation and one root hash computation are performed. This operation is given by Algorithm 6, and its graphical presentation in Fig. 13.
   - *Block Insertion.* An insertion of a new block M_j after block M_i means insertion of the new hash value $h(M_j)$ after the stored hash value $h(M_i)$ and computation of the root hash. This operation is given by Algorithm 7, and its graphical presentation in Fig. 16.

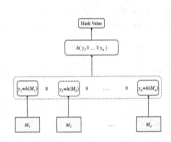

Fig. 12. Incremental hashing using one level tree structure.

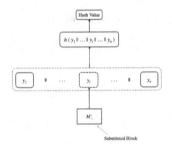

Fig. 13. An update hash operation: Block substitution. Here the block M_i is substituted with the block M_i'.

Algorithm 7 - Block insertion in tree hashing	**Algorithm 8 - Block deletion in tree hashing**
Input. The position i where the insert should be done. The new block M_j and all intermediate leaves hashes $y_1, y_2, \ldots, y_n$.	**Input.** The position i of the block that should be deleted. All intermediate leaves hashes $y_1, y_2, \ldots, y_n$.
Output. $n * k$ bits of leaves hashes and k bits of the root hash.	**Output.** $n * k$ bits of leaves hashes and k bits of the root hash.
1. Calculate $y_j = h(M_j)$;	1. Delete $y_i = h(M_i)$;
3. Concatenate $y_1, \ldots, y_i, y_j, y_{i+1}, \ldots y_n$ and apply h to the concatenated string to get the root hash value $y = h(y_1 \| y_2, \ldots, y_{n+1})$.	3. Concatenate $y_1, \ldots, y_{i-1}, y_{i+1}, \ldots y_n$ and apply h to the concatenated string to get the root hash value $y = h(y_1 \| y_2, \ldots, y_{n-1})$.
4. Output y and store it. Store all the intermediate leaves hashes $y_1, y_2, \ldots, y_{n+1}$.	4. Output y and store it. Store all the intermediate leaves hashes $y_1, y_2, \ldots, y_{n-1}$.

Fig. 14. An algorithm for incremental tree based hash update operation: Block insertion, where the block M_j is inserted after the block M_i.

Fig. 15. An algorithm for incremental tree based hash update operation: Block deletion. Here the block with index i is deleted.

- *Block Deletion.* To delete a block M_i we need to delete the stored hash value of that block and to compute the root hash. It is given by Algorithm 8, and its graphical presentation in Fig. 17.
2. **Data Overhead.** The data overhead is $(n + 1) \times k$ bits which come from n hashes y_i and the final root hash y (Fig. 11).

4   Definition of *i*SHAKE and Security Analysis

Recently, NIST proposed the *DRAFT SHA-3 Standard: Permutation-Based Hash and Extendable-Output Functions* [17], containing definitions for two

Extendable-Output Functions named SHAKE128 and SHAKE256. We just briefly mention their definitions:

$$\text{SHAKE128}(M, d) = \text{RawSHAKE128}(M \,\|\, 11, d), \text{ where}$$

$$\text{RawSHAKE128}(M, d) = \text{Keccak}[256](M \,\|\, 11, d),$$

and

$$\text{SHAKE256}(M, d) = \text{RawSHAKE256}(M \,\|\, 11, d), \text{ where}$$

$$\text{RawSHAKE256}(M, d) = \text{Keccak}[512](M \,\|\, 11, d).$$

iSHAKE128 is the instantiation of the incremental hash function from Algorithm 1 (Sect. 3), where for the hash function h we use SHAKE128 with the output size of 2688 up to 4160 bits. Similarly for iSHAKE256 the output size is in the range of 6528 and 16512 bits (Fig. 14).

Using appropriate values for the time complexity of Wagner's generalized birthday attack (Proposition 1), we have the following:

Proposition 2. *Let for iSHAKE128 parameter $k = 2688$ (for iSHAKE256, $k = 6528$) and let the maximal allowed number of blocks be $N = 2^{25}$ ($N = 2^{28}$ for iSHAKE256). Then*

$$\min_{n \leqslant N} O(n \cdot 2^{\frac{k}{1+\lg\lceil n \rceil}}) = 2^{128.385} \quad (2^{253.103}). \tag{3}$$

By a simple multiplication $b \times N$ we have the following:

Proposition 3. *The lower bound of 2^{128} on the complexity of Wagner's generalized birthday attack on iSHAKE128 for block sizes of 1 KB, 2 KB and 4 KB for the data blocks M_i, can be achieved by hashing files long 32 GB, 64 GB and 128 GB correspondingly. Also for the 2^{256} security bound for iSHAKE256 for block sizes of 1 KB, 2 KB and 4 KB for the data blocks M_i, the hashing files should be long 256 GB, 512 GB and 1 TB correspondingly.*

It is normal to expect that iSHAKE128 would be used for hashing files of size less than 32 GB. In this case there is a tradeoff between the security of finding second-preimage and the size of the hashed files which is expresses by the Eq. (3). For example, for small size files such as 160 KB the complexity of finding second-preimage is 2^{254} and for files of 1.25 TB, the complexity drops down to 2^{112}. Figure 18 shows that trade-off for different file sizes (Fig. 15).

A similar reasoning applies to iSHAKE256 for hashing files of size less than 256 GB. For example for file sizes of 1 MB the complexity of finding second-preimage is 2^{479} and for files of as much as 8 TB the complexity of finding collisions drop down to 2^{212}. Figure 19 shows that trade-off for different file sizes.

If the length of the messages is not restricted, then the low bound security of 2^{128} or 2^{256} in Eq. (3) is achieved for messages with parameter values $k = 4160$ bits for iSHAKE128 and $k = 16512$ bits for iSHAKE256.

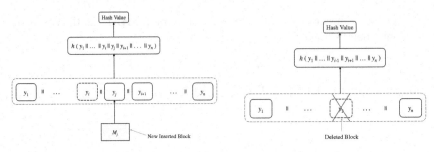

Fig. 16. An update hash operation: Block insertion. Here the block M_j is inserted.

Fig. 17. An update hash operation: Block deletion. Here the block M_i is deleted.

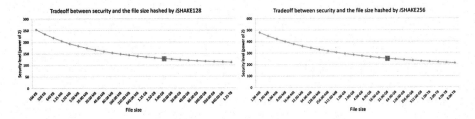

Fig. 18. A trade-off between finding collisions with the Wagner's generalized birthday attack and the size of the hashed file with *i*SHAKE128

Fig. 19. A trade-off between finding collisions with the Wagner's generalized birthday attack and the size of the hashed file with *i*SHAKE256

5   Comparison Analysis

To show the advantages of our new incremental schemes, we compared different performance aspects of our schemes with suitably chosen tree based hashing schemes. We note that a comparison of our approach to a sequential hashing mode does not make sense because it is not parallel and it is not incremental. The only fair comparison would be to schemes with these properties, and currently, tree hashing is the best known method for achieving incrementality. We compared the update effort for different operations and data overhead that introduces additional storage cost. The results in terms of the needed number of operations are given in Table 1.

We also compared the performance in terms of speed of *i*SHAKE and one level tree hashing. Tables 2 and 3 show an evident speed advantage of *i*SHAKE over the corresponding incremental tree hashing of as much as 5 to 6 orders of magnitude. The results in the two tables can be interpreted as follows: For a fixed data overhead for both approaches, what amount of data should be digested in one incremental operation? If we assume an equal digest time per data byte, this can be directly translated into a speed comparison between the two. As an example, consider an input file of size 1 MB. If we use *i*SHAKE128 with blocks of 1 KB, then the amount of bits that we need to store is just the output of the hash

Table 1. Comparison analysis between our incremental hash function approach and tree based hashing.

Incremental hashing scenario	Incremental operation	Update cost	Data overhead	Collision between parallel and sequential hashes
Incremental hashing in fixed size setting	Block substitution	2 data block hash operations	k-bits of hash output $(2600 \leqslant k \leqslant 16000)$	No
Incremental hashing in variable size setting (without migration)	Block substitution	2 data block hash operations	k-bits of hash output $(2600 \leqslant k \leqslant 16000)$	No
	Block insertion	3 data block hash operations		
	Block deletion	3 data block hash operations		
Incremental hashing in variable size setting (with migration)	Block substitution	2 data block hash operations	k-bits of hash output $(2600 \leqslant k \leqslant 16000)$ $+ n \times 64$ bits for the data structure	No
	Block insertion	3 data block hash operations		
	Block deletion	3 data block hash operations		
Incremental tree hashing with a tree depth of 1	Block substitution	1 data block hash operation + 1 hash operation on the intermediate leaves hashes	$n \times k$ bits of intermediate hash values + k bits of final hash output = $(n + 1) \times k$ bits $(160 \leqslant k \leqslant 512)$	Yes [14]
	Block insertion	1 data block hash operation + 1 hash operation on the intermediate leaves hashes		
	Block deletion	1 hash operation on the intermediate leaves hashes		

Table 2. Speed advantage of iSHAKE128 in comparison with SHA3-256 one level tree-based hashing scheme when one block is updated

Fixed data overhead of 2688 bits (iSHAKE128) and 2816 bits (SHA3-256 One Level Tree)											
	1 MB			10 MB			100 MB			1 GB		
Block size in KB	1	4	8	1	4	8	1	4	8	1	4	8
Speed advantage (times)	102.4	25.6	12.8	1024	256	128	10240	2560	1280	104857.6	26214.4	13107.2

function or 2688 bits. If we bound the overhead to the same (or approximate) amount of bits for tree hashing, then we can split the message to a maximum of 10 blocks. In this case, each block will be of size 102.4 KB. Thus, in case we have a change of few (up to several hundreds of bytes) that fall in one block of 1 KB, iSHAKE will rehash only that small block of 1 KB while the tree version of SHA-3 will have to digest significantly bigger block of 102.4 KB. This translates to speed advantage of iSHAKE of 102.4 times.

Table 3. Speed advantage of *i*SHAKE256 in comparison with SHA3-512 one level tree-based hashing scheme when one block is updated

Fixed data overhead of 6528 bits (*i*SHAKE256) and 6656 bits (SHA3-512 One Level Tree)											
	1 MB			10 MB			100 MB			1 GB		
Block size in KB	1	4	8	1	4	8	1	4	8	1	4	8
Speed advantage (times)	85.3	21.3	10.7	853.3	213.3	106.7	8533.3	2133.3	1066.7	87381.3	21845.3	10922.7

6   Conclusion

The need for incremental hashing in the upcoming Zettabyte era is imminent. In this paper, we defined two incremental hash functions *i*SHAKE128 and *i*SHAKE256 with security level against collision attacks of 128 and 256 bits respectively. Both are based on the recent NIST proposal for SHA-3 Extendable-Output Functions SHAKE128 and SHAKE256. We presented constructions for two practical settings: fixed size data and variable size data. In the first one, our proposed scheme has an obvious advantage in the small overhead that it carries out, compared with any other tree-based hash scheme. Moreover, the speed-up is present even in the case where the same data overhead is used. In the second practical setting, our proposed scheme behaves approximately the same as tree based hashing when the dynamic data structure representing the unique identifier of the blocks should be stored. In the case where the unique identifiers of the data blocks are tightly coupled with the media where they are stored, the situation is the same as in the fixed size setting. That is, again, our schemes show much better performance than tree hashing.

We believe that our work will be more than interesting for those practitioners who struggle from using incremental hashing because of the big data overhead that they need to take care of. Therefore, we leave the practical implementation of our newly defined schemes as a future work - one that would possibly focus on some file system and using its structure practically without additional overhead to implement the incrementality of the scheme.

References

1. Amazon web services. An Amazon Company (2015). http://aws.amazon.com/ec2/instance-types/
2. Virtual machine and cloud service sizes for azure. Microsoft (2015). https://msdn.microsoft.com/en-us/library/azure/dn197896.aspx
3. Historical cost of computer memory and storage. hblok.net ● Freedom, Electronics and Tech, February 2013. http://hblok.net/blog/storage/
4. Bellare, M., Goldreich, O., Goldwasser, S.: Incremental cryptography: the case of hashing and signing. In: Desmedt, Y.G. (ed.) CRYPTO 1994. LNCS, vol. 839, pp. 216–233. Springer, Heidelberg (1994)
5. Bellare, M., Micciancio, D.: A new paradigm for collision-free hashing: incrementality at reduced cost. In: Fumy, W. (ed.) EUROCRYPT 1997. LNCS, vol. 1233, pp. 163–192. Springer, Heidelberg (1997)

6. Bertoni, G., Daemen, J., Peeters, M., Van Assche, G.: Sakura: a flexible coding for tree hashing. In: Boureanu, I., Owesarski, P., Vaudenay, S. (eds.) ACNS 2014. LNCS, vol. 8479, pp. 217–234. Springer, Heidelberg (2014)

7. Bertoni, G., Daemen, J., Peeters, M., Van Assche, G.: Sufficient conditions for sound tree and sequential hashing modes. Int. J. Inf. Secur. **4**, 335–353 (2014)

8. Chang, F., Dean, J., Ghemawat, S., Hsieh, W.C., Wallach, D.A., Burrows, M., Chandra, T., Fikes, A., Gruber, R.E.: Bigtable: a distributed storage system for structured data. In: Proceedings of the 7th USENIX Symposium on Operating Systems Design and Implementation, OSDI 2006, Berkeley, CA, USA, vol. 7, p. 15. USENIX Association (2006)

9. Cisco. Cisco visual networking index: Forecast and methodology, 2012–2017. White Paper, May 2013

10. EMC. The EMC Digital Universe study with research and analysis by IDC. Open Report, April 2014

11. Gligoroski, D., Samardjiska, S.: iSHAKE: incremental hashing with SHAKE128 and SHAKE256 for the zettabyte era. In: SHA-3 Workshop (2014). http://csrc.nist.gov/groups/ST/hash/sha-3/Aug2014/documents/gligoroski_paper_sha3_2014_workshop.pdf

12. Hart, J.K., Martinez, K.: Environmental sensor networks: a revolution in the earth system science? Earth-Sci. Rev. **78**(34), 177–191 (2006)

13. Hornby, M.: Review of the best cloud storage services (2015). http://www.thetop10bestonlinebackup.com/cloud-storage. Accessed 01 Mar 2016

14. Kelsey, J.: What should be in a parallel hashing standard? In: NIST, 2014 SHA3 Workshop (2014). http://csrc.nist.gov/groups/ST/hash/sha-3/Aug2014/documents/kelsey_sha3_2014_panel.pdf

15. Merkle, R.C.: A digital signature based on a conventional encryption function. In: Pomerance, C. (ed.) CRYPTO 1987. LNCS, vol. 293, pp. 369–378. Springer, Heidelberg (1988)

16. Mike, S.: How are digital movies distributed and screened? every question answered! http://goo.gl/qLYoIV. Accessed 01 Mar 2016

17. NIST. DRAFT SHA-3 Standard: Permutation-Based Hash and Extendable-Output Functions. FIPS 202, April 2014

18. National Centers for Environmental Information NOAA. Climate Forecast System Version 2 (CFSv2). https://www.ncdc.noaa.gov/data-access/model-data/model-datasets/climate-forecast-system-version2-cfsv2

19. Wagner, D.: A generalized birthday problem. In: Yung, M. (ed.) CRYPTO 2002. LNCS, vol. 2442, pp. 288–303. Springer, Heidelberg (2002)

The Quest for Scalable Blockchain Fabric: Proof-of-Work vs. BFT Replication

Marko Vukolić[✉]

IBM Research, Zurich, Switzerland
mvu@zurich.ibm.com

Abstract. Bitcoin cryptocurrency demonstrated the utility of global consensus across thousands of nodes, changing the world of digital transactions forever. In the early days of Bitcoin, the performance of its probabilistic *proof-of-work* (PoW) based consensus fabric, also known as *blockchain*, was not a major issue. Bitcoin became a success story, despite its consensus latencies on the order of an hour and the theoretical peak throughput of only up to 7 transactions per second.

The situation today is radically different and the poor performance scalability of early PoW blockchains no longer makes sense. Specifically, the trend of modern cryptocurrency platforms, such as Ethereum, is to support execution of arbitrary distributed applications on blockchain fabric, needing much better performance. This approach, however, makes cryptocurrency platforms step away from their original purpose and enter the domain of database-replication protocols, notably, the classical *state-machine replication*, and in particular its Byzantine fault-tolerant (BFT) variants.

In this paper, we contrast PoW-based blockchains to those based on BFT state machine replication, focusing on their scalability limits. We also discuss recent proposals to overcoming these scalability limits and outline key outstanding open problems in the quest for the "ultimate" blockchain fabric(s).

Keywords: Bitcoin · Blockchain · Byzantine fault tolerance · Consensus · Proof-of-work · Scalability · State machine replication

1   Introduction

Distributed consensus, infamous for its limited scalability, was for decades perceived as a synchronization primitive that is to be used only in applications in desperate need of consistency and only among few nodes (see e.g., [8,27]). However, Nakamoto's Bitcoin cryptocurrency [47] demonstrated the utility of decentralized consensus across thousands of nodes, changing the world of digital transactions forever.

Although the Bitcoin protocol does not actually implement consensus in the traditional distributed computing sense, it comes very close to consensus with

© IFIP International Federation for Information Processing
Published by Springer International Publishing Switzerland 2016. All Rights Reserved
J. Camenisch and D. Kesdoğan (Eds.): iNetSec 2015, LNCS 9591, pp. 112–125, 2016.
DOI: 10.1007/978-3-319-39028-4_9

probabilistic agreement [25]. In a nutshell, the goal of a cryptocurrency such as Bitcoin, is to totally order transactions on a distributed ledger, also called a *blockchain*. The Bitcoin blockchain consists of a hashchain of blocks: every block contains an ordered set of transactions and a hash of the preceding block (starting from the initial, the so-called "genesis" block). The key part is the *Proof-of-Work* (PoW) aspect of the hashchain [21]: a Bitcoin block contains nonces that a Bitcoin *miner* (i.e., a node attempting to add a block to the chain) must set in such a way that the hash of the entire block is smaller than a known *target*, which is typically a very small number. In fact, in Bitcoin, the *difficulty* of mining, inversely proportional to the target, is adjusted dynamically throughout the lifetime of the system. The adjustment is made with respect to the block-mining rate and, indirectly, with respect to the computational power of nodes participating in the system, to maintain the expected block-mining rate at roughly one block every 10 min [47]. This latency of 10 min (per block) is often referred to as the *block frequency* (see e.g., [22]) and is one of the two critical "magic numbers" in Bitcoin, the other being the *block size*, which is set in Bitcoin to 1 MB.

In the early days of Bitcoin, the *performance scalability* of its probabilistic PoW-based blockchain was not a major issue. Even today, Bitcoin works with a consensus latency of about an hour (for the recommended 6-block transaction confirmation), and with up to 7 (seven) transactions per second peak throughput (with smallest 200–250 byte transactions). On top of this, the Bitcoin network uses a lot of power, which, in 2014, was roughly estimated to be in the ballpark of 0.1–10 GW [48].

However, blockchain requirements change rapidly, with high latency and low throughput of Bitcoin-like blockchain becoming a major challenge [6]. As a comparison, leading global credit-card payment companies serve roughly 2000 transactions per second on average [58], with a peak capacity designed to sustain more than 10000 transactions per second. Moreover, the trend of modern cryptocurrency platforms, such as Ethereum [57], is to support execution of Turing-complete code on blockchain fabric in the form of *smart contracts*, which are, roughly speaking, custom, self-executing programs (distributed applications) that automatically enforce properties of a digital contract. In fact, smart-contract blockchain is seen as a candidate technology for distributed ledgers in many industries. Clearly, in many of the intended smart-contract use cases, distributed applications require much better performance than that offered by Bitcoin. The banking industry is one prominent example, where potential blockchain use cases go well beyond digital payments [45] to, e.g., securities trade settlements and trade finance.

Smart-contract use cases take the blockchain well beyond its original cryptocurrency purpose, back to the domain of database replication protocols, notably, the classical *state-machine replication* [53]. Indeed, a smart contract can be modeled as a state machine, and its consistent execution across multiple nodes in a distributed environment can be achieved using state machine replication. A family of state-machine replication protocols particularly interesting for blockchain is the family of *Byzantine fault-tolerant* (BFT) [37] state-machine replication protocols, which promise consensus despite participation of malicious (Byzantine) nodes. In more than three decades of research, BFT protocol prototypes have been shown to be practical [10], reaching practically minimal latencies allowed by the network, and supporting tens of thousands transactions per second (see e.g., [3,34]). However, BFT and state-machine replication protocols in general are often challenged for their scalability in terms of number of nodes (replicas) [8], and have not been throughly tested in this aspect critical to blockchain.

In summary, blockchain consensus technologies of today, PoW and BFT, sit at the two opposite ends of the scalability spectrum. Roughly speaking, PoW-based blockchain offers good node scalability with poor performance, whereas BFT-based blockchain offers good performance for small numbers of replicas, with not-well explored and intuitively very limited scalability. This current state of blockchain scalability is sketched in Fig. 1. Given seemingly inherent tradeoffs between the number of replicas and performance, it is not clear today what the optimal blockchain solution is for the sweet spot relevant for many use cases in which the number of nodes n ranges from a few tens to 1000 (or perhaps few thousands).

In this paper, we overview recent efforts towards improving scalability on both sides of the spectrum and highlight interesting directions and open problems in the quest for the "ultimate" blockchain fabric. First, in Sect. 2 we com-

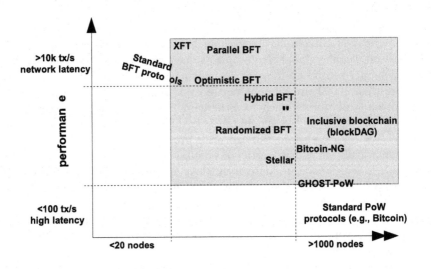

Fig. 1. Illustration of performance and scalability of different families of PoW and BFT protocols discussed in this paper. The actual, real-world performance of systems that touch upon the grey area is subject to further research. Hence, their positioning within the grey area is at the moment entirely speculative and for motivational purposes only.

pare PoW-based blockchains to those based on BFT state-machine replication. Then, in Sect. 3, we overview novel promising approaches to scaling PoW and BFT protocols. We conclude in Sect. 4 with several open questions that will be interesting to tackle in the very near future.

2   PoW vs. BFT Blockchains

Table 1 gives a high-level comparison between PoW consensus and BFT consensus for a set of important blockchain properties. These properties include node identity management, consensus finality (or, dually, the possibility of temporary forks in the blockchain), scalability in terms of number of consensus nodes and clients, performance (latency, throughput, power consumption), tolerated power of adversary, network synchrony assumptions, and, last but not least, existence of correctness proofs of protocols underlying blockchain. This set of properties is certainly not exhaustive, but we believe it is representative for comparing two blockchain families. In the rest of this section, we discuss Table 1 in more detail.

Node Identity Management. How node identities are managed in PoW and BFT protocols is possibly their most fundamental difference. PoW blockchains fea-

Table 1. High-level comparison between PoW and BFT blockchain consensus families for a set of important blockchain properties. Entries in bold suggest desirable features and highlight advantages of one consensus family over the other.

	PoW consensus	BFT consensus
Node identity management	**open, entirely decentralized**	permissioned, nodes need to know IDs of all other nodes
Consensus finality	no	**yes**
Scalability (no. of nodes)	**excellent (thousands of nodes)**	limited, not well explored (tested only up to $n \leq 20$ nodes)
Scalability (no. of clients)	**excellent (thousands of clients)**	**excellent (thousands of clients)**
Performance (throughput)	limited (due to possible of chain forks)	**excellent (tens of thousands tx/sec)**
Performance (latency)	high latency (due to multi-block confirmations)	**excellent (matches network latency)**
Power consumption	very poor (PoW wastes energy)	**good**
Tolerated power of an adversary	$\leq 25\,\%$ computing power	$\leq 33\,\%$ voting power
Network synchrony assumptions	physical clock timestamps (e.g., for block validity)	**none for consensus safety** (synchrony needed for liveness)
Correctness proofs	no	**yes**

ture an entirely decentralized identity management — for example, anybody can download the code for Bitcoin miner, and start participating in the protocol, knowing basically only a single peer to start with. This is a very powerful feature of PoW blockchains and the main reason why they are the blockchain family of choice when it comes to so-called "public" blockchains in which anybody is allowed to participate. Such public blockchains are sometimes also called "permissionless" blockchains — permissionless participation is made possible by PoW, as PoW inherently addresses the Sybil attack [18], infamous in anonymous networks. Specifically, in PoW-based blockchains, the ability of a node (resp., a pool of nodes) to influence the outcome of PoW consensus depends on computational power of a node (resp., a pool).

In contrast, the BFT approach to consensus typically requires every node to know the entire set of its peer nodes participating in consensus. This in turn calls for a (logically) centralized identity management in which a trusted party issues identities and cryptographic certificates to nodes.[1] Intuitively, this aspect of BFT-based blockchains puts it at a disadvantage with respect to PoW blockchains. That said, in a number of emerging blockchain applications (e.g., banking, finance, land and real-estate ownership ledgers) the requirement for known identity of nodes might anyway be imposed for legal and compliance reasons. This explains why BFT consensus protocols are the technology of choice for so-called "permissioned" blockchains, which require blockchain participants identity to be known.

Consensus Finality. Roughly speaking, what is often informally referred to as "consensus finality" (and sometimes as "forward security" [15]) is a property that mandates that a valid block, appended to the blockchain at some point in time, be never removed from the blockchain. In the standard distributed computing terminology, "consensus finality" follows from a combination of the *total order* and *agreement* properties of total order (atomic) broadcast [17], which is the primitive all state-machine replication protocols are built upon (total order broadcast is, in turn, equivalent to consensus). Translated to blockchain terminology, this property can be phrased as follows:

Definition 1 (Consensus Finality). *If a correct node p appends block b to its copy of the blockchain before appending block b′, then no correct node q appends block b′ before b to its copy of the blockchain.*

Consensus finality is not satisfied by PoW-based blockchains. To see why, note that, besides obviating the need for identity management, PoW acts as a randomized concurrency control mechanism, in which the block frequency is adjusted such that block collisions (i.e., concurrent appends of different blocks to the blockchain) are rare. However, as concurrency control is only probabilistic and as block propagation over a network can take some time [16], collisions

---

[1] Here, it is important to note that after an initial bootstrap of a BFT-based blockchain, the nodes already on the blockchain could themselves act together as a distributed trusted party and help reconfigure the system [5,52].

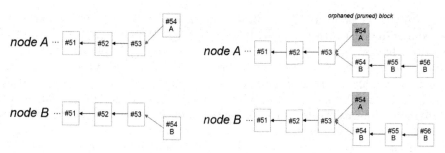

(a) Consensus finality violation resulting in a fork.

(b) Eventually, one of the blocks must be pruned by a conflict resolution rule (e.g., Bitcoin's longest chain rule).

Fig. 2. Illustration of a violation of consensus finality, fork and conflict resolution.

do happen, resulting in temporary forks on the blockchain that PoW-based blockchains are prone to even if all nodes are honest. These temporary forks (see Fig. 2 for an illustration) are resolved by rules such as Bitcoin's longest (most difficult) fork rule [47], or the GHOST rule [54], a variant of which is used in Ethereum. However, the very presence of temporary forks implies no consensus finality. As we discuss in more detail below, absence of consensus finality directly impacts the consensus latency of PoW blockchains as transactions need to be followed by several blocks to increase the probability that a transaction will not end up being pruned and removed from the blockchain (we speak of multi-block confirmation).

In contrast, consensus finality is satisfied by all BFT and state-machine replication protocols.[2] This gives BFT-based blockchains a clear advantage over PoW, as applications, users and smart contracts can have immediate confirmation of the final inclusion of a transaction into the blockchain.

Scalability. Although decoupling the issue of blockchain scalability (with the number of nodes and clients in the system) from that of blockchain performance (latency and throughput) is not entirely possible, we nevertheless first focus on the number of nodes and clients for which PoW and BFT technologies have been proven to work in practice.

On the one hand, the Bitcoin network features thousands of mining nodes, demonstrating node scalability of PoW-based blockchains in practice. That said, it is worth mentioning that grouping of miners into mining pools (with the goal of splitting mining rewards and making mining a financially more predictable endeavour) plagues Bitcoin, effectively centralizing the cryptocurrency [26]. We note that mining pool centralization is not a specific trait of Bitcoin, but more a consequence of the popularity of a PoW blockchain, affecting also many *altcoins* (alternative Bitcoin-like cryptocurrencies) as well as popular blockchains, such as Ethereum.

---

[2] Provided the assumptions about the power of the adversary hold.

On the other hand. BFT and state-machine replication are, in general, perceived as protocols with poor scalability (see, e.g., Brewer's CAP theorem [8]). However, having been invented in the context of replicating traditional applications, such as databases, for fault-tolerance, BFT protocols were never really tested thoroughly for their scalability beyond, say, $n = 10$ or $n = 20$ nodes, in particular in the light of the fairly modest performance targets of many blockchain applications. Intuitively, because of their intensive network communication which often involves as many as $O(n^2)$ messages per block [10], BFT protocols are seen in the database and systems communities as not scalable (see also [44]).[3] This is true even for their crash-tolerant counterparts, i.e., replication protocols such as Paxos [36], Zab [30] and Raft [49], which are used in many large scale systems but practically never across more than a handful of replicas (see e.g., [13]).

Finally, when it comes to scalability with the number of clients, both PoW and BFT protocols support thousands of clients and scale well.

Performance. Beyond the very limited performance of Bitcoin of up to 7 transactions per second (with the current block size) and 1 h latency with 6-block confirmation, PoW-based blockchains face inherent performance challenges. As we already discussed, the two main performance-related parameters of a PoW blockchain are *block size* and *block frequency*. Increasing the block size with the goal of boosting throughput comes at the cost of increasing the latency, because of longer propagation delays of larger blocks across the Internet. These longer delays, in turn, have negative implications on blockchain security: longer delays may increase the number of forks and the possibilities for mounting double-spending attacks [33], because of the possibility of temporary chain forks and absence of consensus finality in PoW blockchains. Similar security challenges apply when the block frequency is increased, with the goal of reducing the latency of multi-block confirmation. The exact security implications of tuning the block frequency and the block size in PoW-based blockchain are in general rather involved (see e.g., [54] for an analysis) and should be handled with care. With this in mind, limited performance is seemingly inherent to PoW blockchains and not an artifact of a particular implementation.

In contrast, modern BFT protocols have been confirmed to sustain tens of thousands of transactions with practically network-speed latencies, not only as prototypes (e.g., [3,12,34]) but also as practical systems [5].

Adversary. PoW and BFT consider different adversaries. In PoW blockchains, what matters is the total computational (hashing) power controlled by the adversary. Initially, Bitcoin was thought to be invulnerable so long as the adversary controls less than 50 % of hashing power. Years later, it was shown that Bitcoin mining is actually vulnerable even if only 25 % of the computing power is

---

[3] That said, it is worth noting that there are *optimistic* BFT protocols with $O(n)$ common-case (expected) message-complexity (see, e.g., [3,51]) — we discuss these later in more detail.

controlled by an adversary [23]. In contrast, BFT voting schemes are known to tolerate at most $n/3$ corrupted nodes [20]. This bound holds only when the network is allowed to be (from time to time) fully asynchronous — strengthening synchrony assumptions makes it possible to raise this threshold. The classical $n/3$ threshold bound for BFT consensus can be generalized to general adversary structures, where an adversary can control different subsets of nodes [28,56].

Network Synchrony. Bitcoin relies on the local time of a node to timestamp a block. Roughly speaking, a block is accepted as valid if its timestamp is greater than the median of the last 11 blocks. Additionally, timestamps play a major role in calculating the difficulty of mining and maintaining block frequency. Therefore, loose clock synchrony is needed for liveness. However, timestamp manipulation attacks that may also compromise the consistency of the blockchain are conceivable (see the "zeitgeist attack" [1]). Although such attacks are difficult to stage against major PoW blockchains such as Bitcoin, they have been successfully performed in the context of some PoW altcoins.

BFT protocols typically do not rely on any physical clock.[4] However, eventually synchronous communication is needed to ensure liveness, owing to the FLP consensus impossibility result, which states that consensus is impossible to achieve deterministically with potentially faulty nodes in a purely asynchronous system [24]. The safety properties of consensus, including consensus finality, are maintained despite global communication outages and arbitrarily long asynchrony periods [20].

Correctness Proofs. Historically, state-machine replication protocols, and in particular their BFT variants, have been recognized as very challenging to design and implement [3,5,11]. Consequently, new protocols are subject to detailed academic scrutiny and therefore come with (more or less) detailed proofs, sometimes even with formal proofs that take an entire PhD thesis (see [14,40]). Even if it may be understandable why Bitcoin was originally deployed without having been subjected to similar scrutiny, it is rather surprising that novel PoW blockchains are rarely accompanied by a detailed security and distributed protocol and security analysis.

3 Improving Blockchain Scalability

In this section we overview and discuss several recent efforts that focus on improving the scalability aspects of both PoW and BFT blockchains.

Improving the Performance of PoW Blockchains. Sompolinski and Zohar recently proposed the GHOST (Greedy Heaviest-Observed Sub-Tree) rule [54], which basically resolves conflicts in a PoW blockchain by weighing the subtrees rooted in blocks rather than the longest (sub)chain rooted in given blocks.

---

[4] Some state-machine replication protocols do use physical clock timestamps, but only to improve performance [19].

Although GHOST is essentially a conflict-resolution strategy, it offers performance benefits over the standard longest (heaviest) chain rule of Bitcoin, as it provides more secure means of increasing the block frequency and the block size [54]. A variant of the GHOST rule is actually implemented in the Ethereum blockchain [57], although the GHOST-PoW performance has not yet been adequately stress-tested with high loads (in 2016, typical Ethereum throughput is fewer than 20,000 transactions per day, i.e., about 0.2 tx/s on average).[5]

Bitcoin-NG is a novel proposal by Eyal et al. [22] that uses standard PoW for leader election, declaring a node which mines a block with standard difficulty (called a key block) to become a leader until a new key block is mined. In the meantime, the leader can append microblocks to the chain, which are not subject to PoW mining but are merely hashchained together. As such, microblocks considerably increase the throughput of the whole system and decrease the latency (that said, Bitcoin-NG is still to be stress-tested in practice). In a sense, Bitcoin-NG mixes leader election, often seen in BFT protocols, with a leader-centric protocol in between leader-election epochs. However, what is different in Bitcoin-NG from BFT protocols is that leader election is PoW-based. Consequently, forks are still possible in Bitcoin-NG and consensus finality is not ensured, which may lead to security implications such as asset double-spending, as discussed earlier.

Scaling Blockchain Through Parallelization. Scaling blockchain by making it a blockDAG (directed acyclic graph) rather than a linear chain of blocks, was recently proposed by Lewenberg et al. in the context of PoW [38]. The idea is to allow non-conflicting transactions (e.g., those transactions that do not constitute double-spending attempts) to be initially on different forks, but to eventually merge the forks by mining a block that would include them both in the ledger.[6] The BFT and state-machine replication communities have also been intensively exploring the idea of *parallel replication* for a few years now, leveraging parallelization of execution of independent requests (transactions) (see, e.g., [32,42]).

Eliminating Communication and Resource Overhead in BFT Protocols. As we have already discussed, the major challenge for BFT protocols that prevents their wider adoption in blockchain is their scalability in terms of the number of nodes. Stellar [43] is an ongoing effort aimed at removing unanimously accepted membership lists from BFT protocols, while maintaining the other BFT advantages over PoW. Other approaches target the BFT scalability without changing membership assumptions. These include *optimistic BFT* protocols [3,51] which feature linear communication complexity in the "common case" and resort to expensive $O(n^2)$ communication among nodes featured by classical protocols such as PBFT [10] only if the network and the process fault pattern are particularly infavorable. However, even optimistic BFT have a resource and communication overhead when compared to crash-tolerant replication protocols (e.g., [30,36,49]), which are better proven in practice and may serve as a baseline for BFT.

---

[5] https://etherchain.org/statistics/basic.
[6] BlockDAGs are conceptually similar to the notion of parallel sharded chains (sidechains) combined with merge mining.

To rectify this, Liu et al. recently proposed a novel network and node fault model called XFT [39] that allows one to tolerate up to $n/2$ Byzantine nodes. At the same time, XFT features message patterns characteristic to crash-tolerant replication protocols, i.e., without the overhead pertaining to typical BFT message patterns. To this end, XFT ("cross" fault tolerance) challenges the established ability of a BFT adversary to control the network and Byzantine nodes simultaneously, decoupling network faults from Byzantine-node faults, treating them as largely independent. As such, XFT goes in the direction of a more realistic adversary model that resembles the one of PoW blockchains, which are not very concerned with the ability of the adversary to control the entire communication network.

Finally, another appealing direction for future BFT-based blockchain is BFT protocols that leverage small pieces of trusted hardware (e.g., [31]) to improve communication and reduce resource cost.

Randomized BFT. Randomized BFT protocols (e.g., [7,9,55]) are appealing alternative to standard, eventually synchronous [20] BFT protocols such as PBFT. Specifically, randomized BFT protocols circumvent the FLP consensus impossibility result [24] by guaranteeing correctness with very high probability (i.e., always, except with negligible probability), rather than deterministically. This allows randomized BFT protocols to be completely asynchronous [4].

For many years, an issue with randomized BFT protocols has been their performance. Specifically, classical randomized BFT (e.g., [4,7,9,55]) are very inefficient compared to eventually synchronous, deterministic BFT protocols mostly due to overhead of cryptographic tools they use. However, this may be changing soon with novel randomized BFT protocols such as HoneyBadger [46] showing promise for good practical performance (i.e., reasonably high throughput) with up to about 100 nodes, through cherry-picking best available cryptographic tools for randomization as well as processing requests in very large batches. Clearly, large batches negatively impact latency, but this could be addressed by *Hybrid BFT* protocols [2] that may combine very efficient optimistic and deterministic BFT protocols (e.g., those described in [3]) with practical randomized protocols such as HoneyBadger. Early examples of such Hybrid BFT protocols can be found in [2,35,51], but the development of future Hybrid BFT protocols can be facilitated by using the modular BFT design framework described in [3].

Mixing PoW and BFT. Recently, Decker et al. [15] have proposed to enhance PoW blockchain with BFT (concretely, the PBFT protocol [10]), primarily to ensure consensus finality in a PoW blockchain by using BFT. SCP [41] also proposes a hybrid PoW/BFT protocol, using PoW for identity management and (parallel and hierarchical) BFT consensus for agreement. Clearly, the above discussion on the importance of scaling BFT in terms of the number of nodes is also critical to such approaches that mix PoW and BFT.

4   Conclusion and Open Problems

We briefly overviewed state of the art as well as emerging directions towards scalable blockchain. We contrasted proof-of-work (PoW) and Byzantine fault-tolerant (BFT) consensus protocols, highlighting their respective advantages.

Future work will be very dynamic and interesting. Making Fig. 1 more precise, i.e., placing various protocols at the correct place with respect to their performance versus their node-scalability, entails a fair amount of research, but represents an immediate open problem that needs to be better understood to facilitate future blockchain scalability improvements. Furthermore, a lot of potential lies in synergies between PoW and BFT, both when it comes to combining protocol techniques and when it comes to refining the adversarial and network models.

Finally, for the most demanding blockchain applications, it would be interesting to move computationally expensive parts of BFT protocols (e.g., cryptography) closer to hardware. In general, implementing consensus in hardware is indeed very appealing and may yield impressive performance, as attested by recent proposals that explore this idea in the context of crash fault-tolerance [29,50].

References

1. The "Zeitgeist attack". http://bitcoin.stackexchange.com/questions/1055/what-is-the-zeitgeist-attack-does-it-affect-all-blockchain-technologies
2. Aguilera, M.K., Toueg, S.: Failure detection and randomization: a hybrid approach to solve consensus. SIAM J. Comput. **28**(3), 890–903 (1998)
3. Aublin, P.-L., Guerraoui, R., Knežević, N., Quéma, V., Vukolić, M.: The next 700 BFT protocols. ACM Trans. Comput. Syst. **32**(4), 12:1–12:45 (2015)
4. Ben-Or, M.: Another advantage of free choice: completely asynchronous agreement protocols (extended abstract). In: Proceedings of the Second Annual ACM SIGACT-SIGOPS Symposium on Principles of Distributed Computing (PODC), pp. 27–30 (1983)
5. Bessani, A.N., Sousa, J., Alchieri, E.A.P.: State machine replication for the masses with BFT-SMART. In: 44th Annual IEEE/IFIP International Conference on Dependable Systems and Networks, DSN 2014, pp. 355–362 (2014)
6. Bonneau, J., Miller, A., Clark, J., Narayanan, A., Kroll, J.A., Felten, E.W.: Sok: research perspectives and challenges for Bitcoin and cryptocurrencies. In: 2015 IEEE Symposium on Security and Privacy, SP 2015, pp. 104–121 (2015)
7. Bracha, G.: An asynchronou [(n-1)/3]-resilient consensus protocol. In: Proceedings of the Third Annual ACM Symposium on Principles of Distributed Computing (PODC), pp. 154–162 (1984)
8. Brewer, E.A.: Towards robust distributed systems (abstract). In: ACM Symposium on Principles of Distributed Computing (PODC), p. 7 (2000)
9. Cachin, C., Kursawe, K., Shoup, V.: Random oracles in constantinople: practical asynchronous byzantine agreement using cryptography (extended abstract). In: Proceedings of the Nineteenth Annual ACM Symposium on Principles of Distributed Computing (PODC), pp. 123–132 (2000)
10. Castro, M., Liskov, B.: Practical Byzantine fault tolerance and proactive recovery. ACM Trans. Comput. Syst. **20**(4), 398–461 (2002)

11. Chandra, T.D., Griesemer, R., Redstone, J.: Paxos made live: an engineering perspective. In: Proceedings of the ACM Symposium on Principles of Distributed Computing (PODC). ACM (2007)
12. Clement, A., Wong, E., Alvisi, L., Dahlin, M., Marchetti, M.: Making Byzantine fault tolerant systems tolerate Byzantine faults. In: Proceedings of the 6th USENIX symposium on Networked systems design and implementation, NSDI 2009, pp. 153–168. USENIX Association (2009)
13. Corbett, J.C., Dean, J., Epstein, M., et al.: Spanner: google's globally distributed database. ACM Trans. Comput. Syst. (TOCS) **31**(3), 8 (2013)
14. de Prisco, R.: On Building Blocks for Distributed Systems. Ph.D. thesis, Massachussets Institute of Technology (1999)
15. Decker, C., Seidel, J., Wattenhofer, R.: Bitcoin meets strong consistency. In: 17th International Conference on Distributed Computing and Networking (ICDCN) (2016)
16. Decker, C., Wattenhofer, R.: Information propagation in the Bitcoin network. In: 13th IEEE International Conference on Peer-to-Peer Computing, IEEE P2P 2013, pp. 1–10 (2013)
17. Défago, X., Schiper, A., Urbán, P.: Total order broadcast and multicast algorithms: taxonomy and survey. ACM Comput. Surv. **36**(4), 372–421 (2004)
18. Douceur, J.R.: The sybil attack. In: Druschel, P., Kaashoek, M.F., Rowstron, A. (eds.) IPTPS 2002. LNCS, vol. 2429, pp. 251–260. Springer, Heidelberg (2002)
19. Jiaqing, D., Sciascia, D., Elnikety, S., Zwaenepoel, W., Pedone, F.: Clock-RSM: low-latency inter-datacenter state machine replication using loosely synchronized physical clocks. In: The 44th Annual IEEE/IFIP International Conference on Dependable Systems and Networks (DSN) (2014)
20. Dwork, C., Lynch, N., Stockmeyer, L.: Consensus in the presence of partial synchrony. J. ACM **35**(2), 288–323 (1988)
21. Dwork, C., Naor, M.: Pricing via processing or combatting junk mail. In: Brickell, E.F. (ed.) CRYPTO 1992. LNCS, vol. 740, pp. 139–147. Springer, Heidelberg (1993)
22. Eyal, I., Gencer, A.E., Sirer, E.G., van Renesse, R.: Bitcoin-NG: a scalable blockchain protocol. In: 13th USENIX Symposium on Networked Systems Design and Implementation, NSDI 2016 (2016)
23. Eyal, I., Sirer, E.G.: Majority is not enough: bitcoin mining is vulnerable. In: Christin, N., Safavi-Naini, R. (eds.) FC 2014. LNCS, vol. 8437, pp. 436–454. Springer, Heidelberg (2014)
24. Fischer, M.J., Lynch, N.A., Paterson, M.S.: Impossibility of distributed consensus with one faulty process. J. ACM **32**(2), 374–382 (1985)
25. Garay, J., Kiayias, A., Leonardos, N.: The bitcoin backbone protocol: analysis and applications. In: Oswald, E., Fischlin, M. (eds.) EUROCRYPT 2015. LNCS, vol. 9057, pp. 281–310. Springer, Heidelberg (2015)
26. Gervais, A., Karame, G.O., Capkun, V., Capkun, S.: Is Bitcoin a decentralized currency? IEEE Secur. Priv. **12**(3), 54–60 (2014)
27. Gilbert, S., Lynch, N.A.: Brewer's conjecture and the feasibility of consistent, available, partition-tolerant web services. SIGACT News **33**(2), 51–59 (2002)
28. Guerraoui, R., Vukolić, M.: Refined quorum systems. Distrib. Comput. **23**(1), 1–42 (2010)
29. Istvan, Z., Sidler, D., Alonso, G., Vukolić, M.: Consensus in a box: inexpensive coordination in hardware. In: Proceedings of the 13th USENIX Symposium on Networked Systems Design and Implementation, NSDI (2016)

30. Junqueira, F.P., Reed, B.C., Serafini, M.: Zab: high-performance broadcast for primary-backup systems. In: Proceedings of the Conference on Dependable Systems and Networks (DSN), pp. 245–256 (2011)

31. Kapitza, R., Behl, J., Cachin, C., Distler, T., Kuhnle, S., Mohammadi, S.V., Schröder-Preikschat, W., Stengel, K.: CheapBFT: resource-efficient Byzantine fault tolerance. In: European Conference on Computer Systems, Proceedings of the Seventh EuroSys Conference 2012, pp. 295–308 (2012)

32. Kapritsos, M., Wang, Y., Quema, V., Clement, A., Alvisi, L., Dahlin, M.: All about Eve: execute-verify replication for multi-core servers. In: Proceedings of the 10th USENIX Conference on Operating Systems Design and Implementation, OSDI 2012, pp. 237–250. USENIX Association (2012)

33. Karame, G.O., Androulaki, E., Roeschlin, M., Gervais, A., Capkun, S.: Misbehavior in bitcoin: a study of double-spending and accountability. ACM Trans. Inf. Syst. Secur. 18(1), 2 (2015)

34. Kotla, R., Alvisi, L., Dahlin, M., Clement, A., Wong, E.: Zyzzyva: speculative byzantine fault tolerance. ACM Trans. Comput. Syst. 27, 7:1–7:39 (2010)

35. Kursawe, K., Shoup, V.: Optimistic asynchronous atomic broadcast. In: Caires, L., Italiano, G.F., Monteiro, L., Palamidessi, C., Yung, M. (eds.) ICALP 2005. LNCS, vol. 3580, pp. 204–215. Springer, Heidelberg (2005)

36. Lamport, L.: The part-time parliament. ACM Trans. Comput. Syst. 16, 133–169 (1998)

37. Lamport, L., Shostak, R., Pease, M.: The Byzantine generals problem. ACM Trans. Program. Lang. Syst. 4, 382–401 (1982)

38. Lewenberg, Y., Sompolinsky, Y., Zohar, A.: Inclusive block chain protocols. In: Böhme, R., Okamoto, T. (eds.) FC 2015. LNCS, vol. 8975, pp. 528–547. Springer, Heidelberg (2015)

39. Liu, S., Cachin, C., Quéma, V., Vukolić, M.: XFT: practical fault tolerance beyond crashes. CoRR, abs/1502.05831 (2015)

40. Losa, G.: Modularity in the design of robust distributed algorithms. Ph.D. thesis, Ecole Polytechnique Federale de Lausanne (2014)

41. Luu, L., Narayanan, V., Baweja, K., Zheng, C., Gilbert, S., Saxena, P.: SCP: a computationally-scalable Byzantine consensus protocol for blockchains. Cryptology ePrint Archive, Report 2015/1168 (2015). http://eprint.iacr.org/

42. Marandi, P.J., Bezerra, C.E.B., Pedone, F.: Rethinking state-machine replication for parallelism. In: IEEE 34th International Conference on Distributed Computing Systems, ICDCS 2014, pp. 368–377 (2014)

43. Maziéres, D.: The Stellar consensus protocol: A federated model for internetlevelconsensus, November 2015. https://www.stellar.org/papers/stellar-consensus-protocol.pdf

44. Mickens, J., The saddest moment. Login Usenix Mag. 39(3) (2014)

45. Milkau, U., Bott, J.: Digitalisation in payments: From interoperability to centralised models? J. Payment Strategy Syst. 9(3), 321–340 (2015)

46. Miller, A., Xia, Y., Croman, K., Shi, E., Song, D.: The honeybadger of BFT protocols. In: Cryptology ePrint Archive 2016/199 (2016)

47. Nakamoto, S.: Bitcoin: A peer-to-peer electronic cash system, May 2009

48. O'Dwyer, K.J., Malone, D.: Bitcoin mining and its energy footprint. In: Proceedings of the 2014 IET Irish Signals & Systems Conference (2014)

49. Ongaro, D., Ousterhout, J.: In search of an understandable consensus algorithm. In: Proceedings of the 2014 USENIX Conference on USENIX Annual Technical Conference, USENIX ATC 2014, pp. 305–320. USENIX Association (2014)

50. Poke, M., Hoefler, T..: DARE: high-performance state machine replicationon RDMA networks. In: Proceedings of the 24th International Symposium on High-Performance Parallel and Distributed Computing, HPDC 2015, pp. 107–118 (2015)
51. Ramasamy, H.G.V., Cachin, C.: Parsimonious asynchronous byzantine-fault-tolerant atomic broadcast. In: Anderson, J.H., Prencipe, G., Wattenhofer, R. (eds.) OPODIS 2005. LNCS, vol. 3974, pp. 88–102. Springer, Heidelberg (2006)
52. Rodrigues, R., Liskov, B., Chen, K., Liskov, M., Schultz, D.A.: Automatic reconfiguration for large-scale reliable storage systems. IEEE Trans. Dependable Sec. Comput. 9(2), 145–158 (2012)
53. Schneider, F.B.: Implementing fault-tolerant services using the state machine approach: a tutorial. ACM Comput. Surv. 22(4), 299–319 (1990)
54. Sompolinsky, Y., Zohar, A.: Secure high-rate transaction processing in bitcoin. In: Böhme, R., Okamoto, T. (eds.) FC 2015. LNCS, vol. 8975, pp. 507–527. Springer, Heidelberg (2015)
55. Toueg, S.: Randomized byzantine agreements. In: Proceedings of the Third Annual ACM Symposium on Principles of Distributed Computing, Vancouver, B.C., Canada, 27–29 August 1984, pp. 163–178 (1984)
56. Vukolić, M.: Quorum Systems: With Applications to Storage and Consensus. Synthesis Lectures on Distributed Computing Theory. Morgan & Claypool Publishers, San Rafael (2012)
57. Wood, G.: Ethereum: A secure decentralised generalised transaction ledger (2015). http://gavwood.com/paper.pdf
58. Zohar, A.: Bitcoin: under the hood. Commun. ACM 58(9), 104–113 (2015)

Author Index

Printed in the United States
By Bookmasters